Db Cooper

The Untold Story of a Daredevil Hijacker

(Chasing the Last Lead in America's Only Unsolved Skyjacking)

Donna Perry

Published By **Bengion Cosalas**

Donna Perry

All Rights Reserved

Db Cooper: The Untold Story of a Daredevil Hijacker (Chasing the Last Lead in America's Only Unsolved Skyjacking)

ISBN   978-1-77485-580-5

No part of this guidebook shall be reproduced in any form without permission in writing from the publisher except in the case of brief quotations embodied in critical articles or reviews.

Legal & Disclaimer

The information contained in this ebook is not designed to replace or take the place of any form of medicine or professional medical advice. The information in this ebook has been provided for educational & entertainment purposes only.

The information contained in this book has been compiled from sources deemed reliable, and it is accurate to the best of the Author's knowledge; however, the Author cannot guarantee its accuracy and validity and cannot be held liable for any errors or omissions. Changes are periodically made to this book. You must consult your doctor or get professional medical advice before using any of the suggested remedies, techniques, or information in this book.

Upon using the information contained in this book, you agree to hold harmless the Author from and against any damages, costs, and expenses, including any legal fees potentially resulting from the application of any of the information provided by this guide. This disclaimer applies to any damages or injury caused by the use and application, whether directly or indirectly, of any advice or information presented, whether for breach of contract, tort, negligence, personal injury, criminal intent, or under any other cause of action.

You agree to accept all risks of using the information presented inside this book. You need to consult a professional medical practitioner in order to ensure you are both able and healthy enough to participate in this program.

TABLE OF CONTENTS

Introduction 1

Chapter 1: Flight 305 10

Chapter 2: Cooper Myth 20

Chapter 3: The Abcs Of The Cooper Case 33

Chapter 4: A Life Well-Traveled 45

Chapter 5: The Many Faces Of D.B. Cooper
.... 63

Chapter 6: Cia So, Are You A Friend Or Foe? 85

Chapter 7: Preparing For Boarding 111

Chapter 8: In The Air To Seattle 116

Chapter 9: The Ground And The Jump . 129

Chapter 10: In The Ground Or In It? 139

Chapter 11: The Case Against 148

Chapter 12: Norjak 166

Chapter 13: A Mystery Continues 178

Introduction

The D.B. Cooper case is among the mysteries that refuse for a solution. It is resistant to any attempts to go beneath the surface to find the answers. The only thing that can be found is more questions.

What other method is there to look at a high-profile crime that has been investigated for more than forty-eight years by state, federal, and local law enforcement officials as well as journalists, scientists and an assortment of amateur detectives but not conclusively in identifying the perpetrator?

After such a long time it's difficult not to be a little skeptical about the whole affair and believe that the mystery cannot be solved. But every year, sane people such as the writer of this book continue to take on the challenge through a tangled and unforgiving rabbit hole, without noticing about the fact that this D.B. Cooper caper could be simply an attempt to make otherwise rational people to the edge, much like legends like the Lost Dutchman's Mine and The Oak Island Mystery before it have been.

My journey into Cooper's world Cooper was not a result of the fact that I was interested in the matter, but rather due to the fact that I had Googled the name of a person and noticed similarity between his pictures and one of the most well-known FBI sketches from Cooper (see Chapter 5). In a spur of the moment I decided to research the suspect, confident that the person couldn't be Cooper in his own right, since if that were the case , surely people prior to me might have noticed the exact similarity to me and confirmed that he was the mysterious skyjacker. As far I could tell the case, my suspect hadn't been noticed by anyone as a possible Cooper or even as an amusing joke. However, the more I looked into the suspect and the more evidence I discovered that suggested he was Cooper himself. Not only did he like the FBI sketch based on the fresh thoughts of the three female stewardesses Cooper had connections to the CIA as well as a past of financial difficulties and parachute-training as well as recent criminal experiences and a love of wearing trench coats and high-ranking associates who could assist him in avoiding his criminal activities. He'd even been in Europe during the time that it was the time that the Dan Cooper comic book was out of print!

In a few ways my investigation into my suspect's background was fairly simple. I had the privilege of researching someone who was a well-known figure within a short time following Cooper's heist, but who also released Cooper Heist but also published no less than three personal memoirs about his adventures. However, I also discovered that due to his inclination to hide the truth, almost everything written by him had to be read with a grain salt and verified and it was difficult to determine what was real and what was not.

While I was immersed in the Cooper investigation, I became horribly aware of something else the majority of what is believed to be true in D.B. Cooper history is in fact incorrect or questioned. Even after all the time since that incident it's hard to sort through all the information and determine what is and isn't true in the incident. What myths are I talking about? One major one is that Cooper demanded that the cash to him in $20 bills and that they not be marked. Cooper did not request that. Also, the money was collected from banks that quickly photocopied the bills, which is a myth that is perpetuated even though there's no way to imagine that a group of people photocopied 10,000 bills, then bundled them together and then transported the bills to the aircraft in about three hours. Instead, the $200,000 was from one bank who had taken the precaution of printing these bills to prevent a criminal from seeking the money. This is a fact that I believe Cooper was aware of.

Then there's the parachutes Cooper employed. One of the stories that keep getting circulated claims that Cooper was initially offered parachutes of the military by McChord Air Force base but turned them down over the possibility of a civilian parachute. The author has found any evidence that this occurred in the transcripts from discussions between the pilots at Cooper at the Sea-Tac airport or in witness statements found in FBI reports. This is because Cooper used an emergency parachute issued by the Navy over the chute that was intended for jumps for recreation. This is an important point.

A lot of the confusion over the investigation stems from the FBI and their files secret until 2007 when they made available certain of the information in 2007 with Citizen Sleuths . There are some details that even the FBI isn't certain of, such as where did the clip-on black tie which could have been belonging to Cooper located? Who was the owner of the parachute Cooper used , and is it one of an NB6 as well as an NB8? How and when did the FBI have to throw away the eight cigarettes butts that they found in the Ashtray Cooper used to fuel the plane? What maps were they of Cooper's request? Cooper wanted to see during the time it was on runway for refueling? And on And onto...

When I could, I made an effort to confirm key Cooper information using multiple reliable sources. To be truly credible, I'd have to access the complete FBI documents that I didn't have access to, and so when I came upon accounts that were not substantiated, I went with the author Geoffrey Gray printed in his investigation of the case, Skyjack the Hunt to Find D.B.

Cooper and observing how he got access to more unredacted FBI documents than any other. In relation to the FBI sketches I was able to inquire about the sketch artist, Roy Rose.

Unsurprisingly, my interest in this case has brought me to the attention of many other issues. For instance,, if you study anything or anyone carefully enough, strange coincidences start to appear. It's at first that these appear to indicate connections however, the more you are aware of the strange-coincidences phenomenon the more convinced you are that random coincidences are just happening. It's fascinating and all however they don't always have any significance. Certain Cooper detectives, for instance are convinced Cooper copied Richard McCoy not only imitated D.B. Cooper but also was Cooper himself. They base much of their claim on the authenticity of credit card accounts that show McCoy was in the area. McCoy resided located in Las Vegas on the day Cooper took over Northwest Orient Airlines. However, even a quick review of the McCoy's files proves that he was too young to be Cooper and, just like others who copied Cooper, was not equipped with the confidence nor the skills to pull off the Cooper theft as flawlessly as Cooper was able to (see the chapter 2.).

The majority of the well-known Cooper suspects possess some peculiarity regarding their background that may make a Cooper novice to believe they are as a valid suspect, however they are not able to overcome the other factors that rule them out. This brings me to a second point I'm compelled make: when it is time to prove or disprove D.B. Cooper suspects Detectives who are amateurs will not eliminate their preferred suspect even when it is clear that the suspect may not possibly have been Cooper. For instance , would the real D.B. Cooper would have been dumb enough to have held up the same airline that he was employed by? Kenny Christiansen's father seems to think so, but never think about the fact that the notion appears to be absurd on the surface .

Naturally, the writer of this article is just as susceptible to the phenomena as the rest of us and is getting ready for the army of critics who are waiting for him. The research he conducted is extensive, but not comprehensive. In the end, he hopes that this suspect will be thought to be plausible by genuine amateur detectives and then proved or rejected.

This is not a guideline on the D.B. Cooper case. If you're looking for the case then you should begin by going through the Wikipedia entry about the case, or read Geoffrey Gray's excellent Skyjack The Search to find D. B. Cooper. (For more in-depth examination of this case read Bruce Smith's excellent D.B. Cooper as well as the FBI The Case Study of the United States' Only Unsolved Skyjacking.) If you don't have time to read all of them books, you can at the very minimum look up Tom Kaye's Citizen Sleuths website. For the moment, I've attempted to list all the bolts and nuts that make up the case.

Refusing to perform its duty and acknowledging defeat and apologizing, the FBI decided to throw its hands up and ended the investigation in the year 2016, which left the taxpayer with a huge bill , and with nothing to show for it. Now it's the other citizens to figure out how to fix this problem.

Chapter 1: Flight 305

November 24 November 24, 1971. 3:00 p.m. Seattle, Washington

"This is 727, isn't it?"

The counter agent turned his attention to the ticket the agent was filling out. "That's correct," he said to the person in front of him , holding the attache bag. "And what would you say your first name"Mr. Cooper?"

"Dan," the other stated, realizing that he'd attracted the attention of others more than had intended. However, sometimes there were mishaps and, considering what he was planning to do it was impossible to risk the possibility that the airline was using an airplane model that wasn't the Boeing 727 without warning.

He sat down in the waiting room and watched the other thirty-six passengers gathered to get on their plane. He remained quiet and sat straight ahead but not in direct view of anyone else even though he scanned them from the edges of his eyes and made notes. A few of them were conversing with one another about the necessity of running off the tarmac during a storm and he wasn't focusing on their conversations. The conversation was, in fact, a source of irritation for him because it seemed so irrelevant, considering the events that were about to unfold. It wasn't their fault however, they appeared to be foolish talking in polite manner as they were about to become part-time players in an upcoming drama developing.

It wasn't helping the fact that his ulcer was throbbing.

When he stepped onto the plane and things settled down, he was able to order an alcoholic drink and relax his nerves. This could help to ease the pain that is gnawing in his stomach for a time.

He smacked the sack of paper lying on the ground with his shoes. In the sack were safety goggles as well as the pair of boots for jumping. The weight of them reassured the man a little. The thermal underwear that covered his legs was not visible from view, however he felt exactly the sameway, and the itching that it caused began to engulf him. Tough. He required extra shield from weather. He'd looked up the weather forecast before the plane landed on the outskirts of Portland and the region they'd be flying over was expected to see a storm and cold temperatures. It would be a nightmare if the plane landed however it would only last for a few minutes. When he finally was on the ground, the temperature would be 40 degrees. It was nothing. He had airdropped earlier into China at a temperature that was lower.

The ticket agent informed the passengers the airplane was now ready to take off along with two young ladies waited at the entrance of the boarding gate onto the tarmac, where the plane was waiting. The man smiled while he sat in his attache case, shocked at how insecure security was. It's no wonder that there's seen a spate of skyjackings during the last 10 years. The situation could change, even if something were to go wrong and one of the passengers subdued the man. If that were to happen, a single telephone call at D.C. and he'd be freed from whatever prison he was thrown into within Seattle with no hassle. The media would be shut down. The flight crew as well as passengers will be instructed to forget about it. The threat of a lawsuit is likely to suffice. If not, the boss will offer a generous payment.

"Dan Cooper" was the next passenger to board the plane to the last. He took a seat in the rear of the aisle seat on the right on the side, facing toward the front. There was no one looking up when he passed however, a neat-cut teenager was in the aisle right next to the seat next to Cooper's. While the child put a suitcase into the compartment above, Cooper sized him up. The boy was tall and was wearing a high school uniform. Maybe he was a football player. It could be a sign of trouble. He'd watch the kid in case it was a hero.

Naturally it's possible that, as Cooper thought of it was, he could be lucky and implement his plan without passengers being even aware. This was the ideal scenario.

He put his attache bag on the window seat vacant right next to him, and stuck the sack of paper and the boots for jumping into the storage compartment underneath the seat directly in the front of him. The flight attendants didn't begin serving drinks until the plane started its flight. Should he have to wait until he'd consumed his drink to decision? That's too late. In any case, he won't really have the need for it. Actually, he wouldn't need it. He'd endured more terrifying experiences than what that he was planning to endure. There were many more. As always, he did this to help his country.

Mostly.

If he succeeded or not the heist was bound to cause a stir. In the aftermath, airlines would be forced to increase the security of their flights. Nobody should be able to sneak in an explosive, or fake bombs. Many skyjackings led to a fruitcake being smuggled onto the plane towards Cuba. The incident ended today.

A flight attendant explained the safety guidelines. The engines then started to crank up. He didn't seem to be worried anyhow. He was just excited. Two months prior at the beginning of more than a decade, he'd gotten on the most recent of his capers. Setting the plan in motion, getting his comrades in Miami traveling across the country to California as well as snooping into the medical office to search for dirt - all of it was a way to rejuvenate his. He's never been an in-demand adrenaline addict. How many people are willing to serve three tours of military duty in an entire conflict?

The saga of two months earlier had produced nothing of value. However, orchestrating it and being able to escape the crime was awe-inspiring! It was also during the lengthy flight back D.C. that he'd hatched the idea to pay for the Agency for its treatment of him as well as instruct his bosses in how to handle problems like hippies taking over planes and requesting to be transported to Cuba. If everything were as they were supposed to be--he'd come out with enough cash to pay for those huge medical bills his daughters accumulated, as well as a couple of dollars more. Perhaps enough to purchase an all-new car. The whole thing could be prevented had the Agency did the right thing and looked after him.

When the plane sped off the runway, the pilot glanced at the boy in the middle of the row, staring through his window. It's likely he'd be fine. "Dan Cooper" knew how to deal with youngsters. In addition to being a teenager himself He also had four kids. The oldest probably was exactly the same age as the boy. Cooper was a man with a look that could cause his children to fall apart as they grew smarter with Cooper.

He settled down in his seat while a beautiful brunette-haired flight attendant strolled to the aisle, accompanied by an alcohol cart. Cooper took a 7-Up drink and Bourbon. Cooper would have preferred a decent Scotch, but it was one of the things he was famous for, and he didn't want to take the chance that someone might remember that and link the dots. And he was missing his pipe. He'd left it in the house as he was famous for his pipe. Instead, he'd bought the pack of Raleigh cigarettes at the airport.

He attempted to pay for his drink with twenty-dollar bill, but the waitress could not break it, so she advised him to come back later with his cash. He didn't think a thing about the change and the idea that he'd require money following the events he'd planned , made him realize that the time was now.

Cooper took an envelope out of his coat pocket inside and held it in front of her. In a blank stare, she removed her envelope and...put it back in her coat pocket.

"Miss," he said in a calm, but urgent tone, "I think you'd better take a look at that now."

She took her envelope out, opened up, and then read the note inside, her face changing to an attractive white.

She sat down, obscuring her from the gaze of the young man in the opposite aisle. "Is this true?" she whispered.

He smiled and pointed towards the attache case using his thumb.

"Show me your bomb,"" she saidwith the phrases getting stuck the inside of her mouth.

While unable to move the casing, he detached the fasteners, then opened it to reveal six red cylinders as well as some wiring. Her mouth was covered with hands, and backpedaled.

He concluded the case.

"You'd better notify all pilots to be aware," he said, looking towards the aircraft's front. "And we'll keep this among the pilots and my crew is that okay?" He'd already put it in the memo but it's not a bad idea to remind her.

She nodded and then walked along the aisle with a furious grin as she slammed into a few seats as she left the cabin.

He realized it was the time to put the sunglasses on. He'd intended to put them on before that he stepped off the plane. This was the only error that he'd made.

He took the sunglasses out of the pocket of his shirt and put them into. It could be odd to passengers around him, wearing sunglasses in an airplane with dim lighting. But they'd figure out a reason to justify it and say that he suffered from vision issues or wanted to sleep and block out as much of the ambient light as they could.

People were always filling the blanks. It's human nature. Most of the time, they filled in those gaps incorrectly, causing confusion and causing problems. This could help his cause.

Dan Cooper. He spoke the words, and the melody of them was pleasing to him. It was a straightforward name, and simple to remember. He was already a fan of it over his various aliases that he'd employed in the past when he worked for the Agency and also in his personal writing career as a novelist. Robert Dietrich, Walter Twicker, Gordon Davis, David St. John, Eduardo Hamilton, Hugh Newstead, Edward Warren -- these were only a few of the names he'd chosen to conceal his identity however the real name was Everett Hunt. The people he hung out with called him Howard and in the professional world, many people referred to him by his name of E. Howard Hunt, which was somehow more powerful and was more fitting for one employed by the most powerful person in the world.

Who was the President Richard Nixon.

Chapter 2: Cooper Myth

Thank you dear reader, for not throwing your e-reader into the air when you reached the last paragraph in the chapter before. In the past were I to have read those paragraphs, a good quantity of eye-rolling would've been evident. I'm sure I'd be having a hard time being convinced that a member from the Nixon administration was responsible for an infamous and famous crimes in the history of heists. Why should a man who'd worked for 20 years with the CIA and was a director in the White House risk everything in an extremely publicized heist to steal $200,000? The physical resemblance isn't the only thing that makes him a Hunt isn't a great potential candidate for the famed skyjacker.

It's also because, just a few days after the Cooper heist occurred it was revealed that D.B. Cooper was an everyday man sort of Joe who devised an innovative plan to make a profit and give it back to the establishment. Cooper wasn't a mastermind , but just a normal guy struggling to make ends meet who was determined to extort money from an airline company because of desperation or a desire to get revenge.

This false belief is the reason most of those most admired D.B. Cooper candidacies were actually non-assuming people from common backgrounds, such as Uncle L.D. Cooper, Robert Richard Lepsy as well as Kenny Christiansen. Many D.B. Cooper fans were enthralled by the idea of the fact that Cooper did something that he actually could have accomplished, were the motivation there.

However, a quick examination of the investigation reveals that, whoever Cooper was an individual, he was not typical. It could be that the heist was carefully designed by someone who had prior experience with similar operations or Cooper had a chance beyond imagination.

For instance:

1. Cooper happened to board the only airliner model that was in operation at the time capable of lowering its stairs in mid-flight this was a fact that was not well-known to the general population.

2. Cooper instructed the pilot to fly at the right speed and altitude to permit someone to unlock the staircase in mid-flight, and then lower the stairs and airdrop safely.

3. Cooper somehow smoked eight cigarettes and did not leave marks on the butts in the Ashtray.

4. Cooper happened to pick the city where a bank had $200,000 in cash waiting to be taken by the outlaw who got the money first.

5. Cooper either landed safely or slid to his death , with no body, briefcase or parachutes being discovered, despite months of search by bloodhounds, military personnel and, at the very least, a CIA surveillance plane.

6. If Cooper was able to land safely, there were nobody was able to testify at the time of the incident to witnessing Cooper stumbling out of the woods with a bag of money. (Decades later, when it wasn't a big deal witnesses who were doubtful said they had seen Cooper in the form of a hitchhiker, or witnessed him go into an eatery after the incident.)

7. The Cooper bills were ever discovered in circulation.

8. Although it was viewed by a total of fifteen witnesses (some of whom sat for time with him) The FBI artist's rendition based on the testimony of these witnesses failed to identify any person the FBI believed to be a plausible suspect.

9. Apart from the cigarette ash and two hairs that were found on the seat's rest and the parachutes that were not used the only evidence Cooper might have left behind at the time of the crash was the tie that could be a deliberate choice or belonged to an entirely different passenger.

10. If Cooper lived, he wouldn't have boasted about the crime to anyone who complained to authorities, despite an offer of $25,000 in reward provided by the airline company Cooper took advantage of.

11. No matter if Cooper survived or died after the beginning The FBI was unable to resolve the mystery after 45 years of searching.

All dumb luck? Unlikely.

And Cooper isn't exactly the average Joe when looking at his heist in relation to similar attempts by others to replicate the feat, none of which was successful. The most famous was performed the by Richard McCoy, who committed his skyjacking just four months following Cooper's. But while Cooper executed his operation in a calm and calm manner and did not draw any attention, McCoy's scheme appeared like something straight from the bad Jim Carey movie.

McCoy who was an ex- Green Beret and experienced parachutist who had studied security at airlines and even wrote a dissertation on the topic for a class in which he was enrolled in Brigham Young University. Prior to attempting the heist and planning the entire operation, he had laid it out, and had modeled much of it on Cooper's plan, however once he put his plan into operation, he fell off almost every aspect of it. First, he had typed out instructions in writing on paper slips which he was planning to hand over on to his flight attendants however, when the day of the heist came around, McCoy left the envelope with the notes at the ticket counter prior to boarding the plane. (Fortunately for the flight attendant, she was able to retrieve the envelope and return that envelope back to McCoy without ever opening it.)

On the plane after landing, he went into the bathroom to put on his costume. In an effort to hide the size of his ears, he put an unfit wig on his head. But the hair would not cooperate. when he attempted to get the hair to remain in position by pouring water over it, black pus ran over his face. The disguise took too long in putting on, that one flight attendant was required to knock against the doors of the bathrooms in order for McCoy to leave the tiny chamber before the plane could begin its journey.

When McCoy was finally able to leave the toilet His uncharacteristic behavior caused suspicions among the attendants and the passengers who informed the pilots the passenger was being oddly. The pilots switched their planes towards the closest airport, and called the FBI to ensure agents would be waiting in the ground.

When the captain made a decision to change the plan of travel, McCoy realized the jig was over and took out an unintentional hand grenade and declared he was the one who had taken over the plane. He then prompted one of the passengers to grab the camera and take the head shot of McCoy hoping to get an image that could be sold to magazines.

Like Cooper, McCoy had taken the extra precaution of bringing on his own parachutist for the jump however, when he took it from the overhead compartment the rip cord pulled in a way, and the parachute flew from its case, hitting into the stewardesses, and almost injuring her.

Amazingly, despite all the chaos, McCoy did manage to successfully to demand his ransom, get his money, and even drop out of the plane however, unlike Cooper in this case, he left fingerprints, handwriting samples and a photograph of himself in the background.

Witnesses said he fell through the woods and trying to hitchhike.

The next day, the FBI was able to arrest him.McCoy's most costly mistake? not realizing that Cooper was able to pull off an extremely complicated robbery style easy, the same mistake all the other Cooper replicators would all make.

There were numerous. There were at least 15 according to the writer Malcolm Gladwell. If one examines the details about their crimes, one consistent theme emerges: they were all royal mishaps. This is why they were swiftly caught. Consider:

* Richard Charles LaPoint, one of the first Cooper copycats. With no experience in parachuting the thief took over the 727 using fake bombs demanding $50,000 as well as two parachutes, and was rescued in the northern region of Colorado. Following a sprain to both his ankles on his landing arrested by authorities after they found his footprints in the snow.

* Robin Dolin Heady, who stole $200,000 after snatching a 727 from Reno and jumping out into darkness close to Washoe Lake. The authorities arrested him after they discovered his getaway vehicle in the vicinity of the lake. The tip-off? It's the United States Parachute Association sticker placed on the car's bumper.

* Billy Gene Hurst, an Oklahoman who took control of the flight between Houston in Texas to Dallas. When the plane arrived, Hurst let the 94 passengers aboard go for free but he held on to passengers and flight staff and demanded a variety of things, including $1,000,000 cash, eight lunch boxes and the parachute. In violation of one of the rules for hijacking Hurst did not see the remaining hostages as he began to examine the parachute. He then allowed members of the crew get away from the airplane. The police rushed onto the plane and arrested Hurst.

* Martin McNally, winner of the award for the best funny Cooper replica heist. In a purple-lensed wig and wig, glasses, the 28-year-old McNally was able to sneak a submachine gun inside a trombone case aboard a 727. He then commandeered aircraft in Tulsa and demanded that the plane be diverted towards St. Louis. After arriving, he demanded $500,000. In at the St. Louis airport, one of the passengers who was angry at the television coverage from the lounge at the airport, jumped onto his spouse's Cadillac convertible and jumped on

the 727 waiting for him before crashing into the front wheel of the car and completely wrecking the vehicle. McNally switched to a new 727, and had the plane transferred to Indiana and then jumped off to the landing area. Not having any experience with parachuting and no experience, he jumped in the air at random prior to opening his chute in such a manner that it crashed into his face. While he was preparing to, he witnessed the money bundle which he'd secured to his body swoop free and fall through the clouds, disappearing away from his grasp for ever. An analysis of his fingerprints led to his arrest days later.

In comparison, Cooper looks better and more attractive. He clearly was trained and experienced in performing covert operations under a lot amount of stress. In all of that, the issue that must be addressed is what was the way that the D.B. Cooper-was-a-regular-guy legend ever take root?

You can blame it on the FBI.

When the heist took place in the early days, the FBI was cautious with a lot of the details in hopes that by keeping the details vague, they'd be able to differentiate the fraudulent Cooper suspects from the likely suspects after they were exposed. It was not until after the Vietnam War ended years later when Americans became aware of the agency's Air America campaign involving Boeing 727s that were used to drop agents and cargo onto foreign territories, such as Cambodia in Cambodia and Laos. The ability of the 727 to lower its aft stairs during flight made it the perfect aircraft for this particular mission. This bit of knowledge helped Cooper appear a little more unique.

Also, he instructed his pilot that he fly the aircraft at 10,000 feet with flaps on the wings lowered by 15 degrees, landing gear up at speeds of 100 knots. This was something that suggested Cooper was pilot and/or had experience in airdropping cargo from 727s.

Inadvertently accidentally, the FBI caused other issues, as well. From the beginning they believed that Cooper was killed in the leap. The weather conditions were terrible and Cooper was able to jump in the night. He was also carrying a load of twenty pounds of loot . He landed in the wilderness. As months turned into weeks and Cooper was not discovered alive, the public assumed that the FBI was right and Cooper had died during the attempted. The accepted narrative was that Cooper was not prepared for the last action. Cooper had thought of the most bizarre method of robbing the victim hundred of thousands. But he had not considered the risky scenario it would be to leap off an aircraft at night in an erupting rainstorm.

In the end, Cooper became an iconic folk hero. In the end, not just had the passengers on the 727 were wounded, but the flight crew that met with reporters shortly after the heist looked unflappable and not much less than. Based on the reports of the Stewardesses Cooper was courteous and well-spoken throughout the heist, and a gentleman's bandit. Furthermore Cooper was clean cut, well-dressed and respectful. He even set up for the crew of the flight to eat dinner while the plane was on runway at Seattle Airport, for refueling. He was increasingly taking on the John Dillinger or Jesse James persona.

As time passed and Cooper did not have a name and unknown, it was less likely that he was a career criminal. After all, in the event that he had a criminal record, there were fingerprints in the files of the FBI to verify with the fingerprints that they located, or even mug photos that would have allowed people who witnessed the incident to I.D. Cooper, or have an established method of operation that the police could be able to recognize.

There was also that whole grudge issue. In one instance on the way to Seattle an attendant on the flight Tina Mucklow asked Cooper why the reason he was angry with the airline. Cooper was reported to have replied, "I don't have a grudge with your airline, Miss. However, I do have an issue." Perhaps Cooper was not even interested in the cash. In the end, it appeared to be like he was a normal person who was delivering retribution after being taken advantage of to the tune of the government.

Many people were hoping Cooper survived and got away.

He did this for seven months in all likelihood. But then karma snuck up on him in a huge way.

Chapter 3: The Abcs Of The Cooper Case

The attraction of having a contemporary folk hero among them wasn't the sole reason Americans were fascinated with this Cooper heist. The crime itself was a bit bizarre and gruesome. Cooper's extraordinary poise during the five hours in the air seemed strange, and his attire -- dark professional suit with loafers black trench coat, and those glasses--sounded odd, considering his plan to jump from a plane at night , and with 7 degrees Celsius (factoring into windschill). Why wouldn't he wear winter clothing, boots, and an oversized ski cap? He wouldn't have looked with the other passengers?

His clothes weren't the sole thing that didn't add up. The FBI wanted to find someone with the need for money in a hurry or, for instance, who had a huge gambling debt he wanted to pay off, but that didn't seem to make sense at all. If someone is in need of money quickly and urgently, he will rob an institution. He doesn't have a plan for an elaborate scheme that includes hostages, a bomb or a hostage or ransom cash that the airline may or might not pay or pay, a skyslide and the apparent execution of a plan of escape after he's landed. It is also possible considering that Cooper was in control throughout the entire process and how he was able to manipulate him to have his plane fly directly over the region where he intended to jump, without being able to make it clear. All of this will require a lot of planning, which will require time. Days, perhaps weeks at the minimum an option that someone in need for money probably doesn't have.

What about the offer that was made by Cooper of $200,000? What was the reason for that number? It could be an unpaid betting debt. Or perhaps Cooper knew that $200,000 was a reasonable amount to request. According to FBI reports, it is the case that prior to the Cooper leap it was reported that it was reported that the First National Bank of Seattle had set aside and printed $230,000 in the 20th century to ensure that should someone steal their bank the serial numbers were already registered. Did Cooper somehow privy to this information?

Given all this is why it's so surprising that the FBI ever believed Cooper was a common criminal. Then again, it's true that the FBI investigation was mishandled from the start and at times, it appeared that the FBI was a partner in the skyjacking.

The last person to meet D.B. Cooper during the Heist was the Stewardess Tina Mucklow. Mucklow also spent the most time with him, sat beside him for the majority of the flight of two hours to Portland until Seattle. After Cooper was paid, she released him after releasing the hostages and then left with the 727 with the flight crew , heading towards Reno, Nevada (where the plane would refuel prior to taking off for Mexico), Cooper asked Mucklow to guide him on how to lower the stairs to the forward of the plane. After this she locked herself into the cockpit along with the other flight crew members while leaving Cooper to himself at back of the aircraft until he was able to jump out.

The investigation started when the plane came in to Reno. The flight crew were fairly certain Cooper had jumped out of the plane mid-flight. One pilot had observed an abrupt reduction in air pressure after the aft-door indicator light went on which indicated the exact moment Cooper had made his leap. The question was still about whether there was a bomb in the plane and, as soon as the plane landed on the runway, Mucklow returned to the cabin at the rear and surveyed the area that Cooper was seated, looking for the bomb.

She was able to locate two of the parachutes Cooper requested however, she didn't find the attache case that contained the bomb. (She did not look at the tie Cooper claimed to have left behind, which leads one to ask whether it was actually evident on Cooper's car, which some have claimed.)

After the flight crew left the plane and the FBI began to swarm aboard, searching the back cabin for clues, and searching all over the 727 to make sure Cooper was not still in the plane, in hiding.

The FBI discovered the black narrow tie that some claimed Cooper was wearing, the butts of cigarettes Cooper consumed, as well as two brown hairs on the headrest that belonged to the seat where Cooper was sitting. The glass Cooper used to sip his seven-ups and two bourbons was not present. (Some claim that it was just a single drink but it wasn't two.) Cooper was either throwing it off in the air or mixed it with other glasses of passengers an act one wouldn't expect someone with no experience to imagine doing. A palm print was found from the steps in front, however it was difficult to determine whether it was left by Cooper or somebody else.

Then the FBI interrogated witnesses. This is where the initial impression was that it was unusual.

As a man who kept 36 passengers captive with the appearance of a bomb Cooper was a man with a ability to go under the radar. Although the majority of passengers and flight crew estimated his age as mid-forties two passengers estimated him to be in his 30s, and another put him in his early 50s--a pretty wide variety. Many people remember Cooper wearing an all-black suit, while others recall him wearing have brown (or russet) and pin-striped. The color of his hair was described in various ways as brown or jet-black. The majority of witnesses believed that he was Caucasian however, the Flight agent Florence Schaffner and one of the passengers believed they were Latino. Some passengers believed they were olive skinned while others believed he was just thin. The theories about his height varied between 5 9" to 6'1". Schaffner was the only person to look at his eyes and this was when he handed her the note that warned her to the fact that he was carrying the bomb. After that, he donned glasses.

The differences in testimony of witnesses can be explained by looking at how the light conditions were and also seating arrangement in the airplane. The flight occurred in the afternoon, which means that most of the lighting was likely to have come from cabin lights of the airplane, so it could be somewhat dim. Cooper was seated in the back in the back of the airplane. Only one of the passenger (William Mitchell) was seated on his left. After Cooper announced his plans to the crew of the flight and the attendants, they took all passengers, with the exception of Cooper three rows higher which meant that fewer passengers were able to have a close view of Cooper and did not get a reason to look at Cooper's face.

The FBI put off the investigation for two days following the heist, which gave Cooper the chance to get a head start. The FBI didn't wish to launch a helicopter search in the suspected jump area until the winter storm had gone, and no one would want to stomp across the ground under those conditions, not having an idea of the location Cooper was able to jump.

Furthermore, even at an early stage authorities from law enforcement believed Cooper was a runner into the air and died So why would they rush to locate a body?

The FBI did not believe that Cooper did not make it to the top because in their eyes , he was unsure of the procedure he was following. Cooper was given four parachutes from which to choose however he'd picked an dummy chute to use as a backup (the person who given the chutes to police had handed over the dummy chute accidentally) and he'd picked the difficult-to-read military chute instead of the sports parachutes, which indicated that he wasn't an expert. Additionally, he'd leapt out in complete darkness, without any lighting source (as as they could tell) and was wearing clothes totally inappropriate for winter conditions. They also asked at the time if it was feasible for someone to leap from the aft of the stairs without injury.

In discrediting Cooper as a badly prepared criminal the FBI did not consider the numerous things Cooper did correctly. These details would become apparent when Cooper's copycats Cooper replicators went down in fires in such a way and the FBI would not admit that Cooper likely knew the details of what Cooper was doing from beginning to the end.

However police officials responsible for the Cooper investigation weren't willing to take any risks. The Cooper incident was the talk of the town--even CBS anchor Walter Cronkite had included a mention in his evening broadcast -- and they didn't want to let Cooper be able to get away with the criminal act. After the heist, Cooper was arrested, the FBI as well as local authorities started looking for the location which eventually led to the arrival of thousands of troops from the military to assist for a period of weeks, and then months. However, there was no trace or evidence of Cooper or the cash was discovered until nearly nine years later when the eight year old Brian Ingram stumbled across $6,000 of it in a bank near the Columbia River, twenty miles from the suspected site of the jump.

Theorists speculated that Cooper was a swan who fallen into one of the lakes and then tangled in his parachute and then drowned. One investigator even hired an underwater vessel and searched one of the lakes however, he was no more successful than the other researchers.

Another possibility is that some fortunate person found Cooper's remains and loot, even though nobody else was present and then dumped Cooper's body and ran off with the cash. It's unlikely as the person who discovered the money might have had difficulty explaining to his family and friends the source of the money and he'd have to either launder the money or invest it in a manner that no one could have matched the serial numbers to the list provided by the U.S. Attorney General provided.

However, it might be a little easier considering the way in which the figures were distributed to the general public.

A few weeks after the heist The Attorney General at the time John Mitchell released the Cooper bills serial numbers to law authorities, banks with large amounts of money and casinos. Two issues surfaced immediately. One was that there was the fact that Cooper bills all in the twenties and were a standard bill that circulated back in the era of prohibition, so it could have been difficult for banks or casinos to look through every Cooper bill they received. There were so many numbers recorded to look through that there were 10,000. Perhaps a shrewd bank or casino would try its best to verify for twenties each time they came in, but what length of time? Absolutely Cooper was aware that the serial numbers were released, and he therefore had every reason to keep the cash until the heat went down.

In January, the Attorney General made available the bill's serial numbers to the public at large. Two papers (one in Oregon and the other in Washington) decided to release the numbers. FBI documents show that Portland Journal printed the numbers in three separate issues in three issues. To further encourage readers the Journal provided a cash reward of $1,000 to the first person who returned any of the Cooper bills. However, normally, when law enforcement agencies issue serial numbers to the general public, they don't issue them all at once. There were few who took the trouble of studying each bill they received and, If Cooper was not spending funds within the Pacific Northwest, it's not any surprise that nobody could match one of the bills to the list of bills published by only two newspapers.

In February, the military become increasingly desperate to locate Cooper (or his body) and so they flew their SR-71 Blackbird spy plane over the area of search in hopes to locate traces from the skyjacker. It also was a failure.

Then, when the FBI looked into the small black tie Cooper claimed to have had left, they discovered that it came made by J.C. Penney. The tie was then taken into J.C. Penney's corporate headquarters located in Chicago and were told the tie was sold in bundles and was mostly for employees of the service sector, such as busboys or waiters.

It is unlikely that Cooper was a busboy.

Chapter 4: A Life Well-Traveled

It is believed that the name E. Howard Hunt is immortalized in the minds of those who were affected by that Watergate scandal. In fact it is so well-known, it is even the Ethan Hunt character Tom Cruise portrays on Mission Impossible. Mission Impossible movies was reputedly named after the former Nixon plumber. While many Americans are familiar with his name, a few know much about the man. So who did E. Howard Hunt?

In 1918, in Hamburg, New York, nothing about his childhood indicated that someday his name would be featured on top spot at the top of the newspapers all over the globe and that he'd be engaged in two or three crucial events during the latter period in the Twentieth Century. In this boy from a small town was an unquenchable desire for adventure, and that when World War II broke out The recently graduated Brown University grad wasted no time in joining the Navy. He was an officer on a destroyer before the time he suffered a groin injury, which led to a medically discharge.

Hunt was then able to spend the following period writing thought to be the very initial World War II novel published by a veteran. East of Farewell, a naval action novel that was admired for its authenticity. The novel attracted the attention of a film maker, and, before long, Hunt was an author for March of Time newsreels. After that, he was offered an unintentional stint as a war correspondent at Life Magazine, a desultory time for a budding writer. The station was in South Pacific, where he sometimes flew on bomber flights. In the South Pacific the pilots of his friends were teaching Hunt how to fly land and sea planes. Hunt gained enough proficiency that he could regularly pilot the planes to go on alcohol runs. It's no surprise that he learned much about aviation during that time which explains why his alter ego appeared to be to be so well-informed when he gave instructions for flying to a terrified flight crew 26 years later. Then Hunt got tired of his work for Life and returned to the Army with the Army Air Corp.

Unfortunately for Hunt the military decided that he'd previously completed two tours within the South Pacific, so they declined his request to go overseas and instead, they placed him at the location within Orlando, Florida.

Wanting to take part in the war at an active basis, he applied to join the OSS (Office of Strategic Services) The wartime intelligence agency founded in 1941 by the General William Donovan in 1941. An early predecessor to the CIA the OSS was famous for its method of dropping agents in the midst of enemy lines and often in complete darkness. The OSS's training camps were established in National Parks located in the close vicinity of Washington, the capital of the United States. According to the website of the National Park Service, "candidates were chosen based on a mix of intellect, imagination creativeness, courage and ruthlessness" qualities that many later consider to be the work of D.B. Cooper. The program was modeled on British Special Operations, and students were taught items as using guns, lock-picking, as well as parachuting. They also received many hours of parachuting training. Starting from the close Quantico air base, the trainees would leap into the parks at least five times during the course of a single day.

Hunt was admitted to the Agency and was a part of the gruelling training course. In his memoir, Hunt notes that a part of the program involved the recruits being forced to live on the open plains of the desert for an entire week by relying on their abilities and the tools they came up with and skills that would prove valuable should someone decide to plunge into the thick North Pacific wilderness while toting the cash worth $200,000.

Following the end of the war, Hunt won a Guggenheim Fellowship and then briefly recommenced the writing profession. However, his love of adventure was calling out to Hunt, and in 1949 Hunt joined the CIA. In France and then in France, he got to know his future wife, who was an American divorced woman working with the Agency as secretary.

In the year 2000, Hunt's most popular novel was released, Bimini Run. A Hollywood studio bought it for $5,000 hoping to make it film, however this didn't come to fruition. The matter was irrelevant. At that point,

Hunt was firmly ensconced within the Agency. In 1950, he was made the station's chief of staff at Mexico City, a town that is famous for among others, the smuggling of money. (Twenty years afterward, D.B. Cooper would instruct pilots that they should fly into the city, and he would hijack their aircraft.)

After a brief period within Mexico City the Hunt family relocated to Japan and then Uruguay. While in both states, Hunt helped orchestrate the removal of the democratically elected President from Guatemala, Jacobo Arbenz, who had made the mistake of collaborating with United Fruit Company, a subsidiary of the US-based United Fruit Company and being in favor of Communism.

A few years later, when the CIA was pursuing Fidel Castro, Hunt was given the task of forming the new government to be in charge following his Castro regime was thrown out the exit. As he explains in his memoir of 1974, Give Us this Day This was primarily about Hunt's endeavor to keep the competing parties of Cuban exiles in peace. If he wasn't mediating conflicts between the two groups, he was also spending time in Guatemala in a CIA-funded training camp for exiles that would later be part of the war. When he returned to the States he was operating in a safe residence in Miami. Cuban Exile Bernard Barker was assigned to serve as his personal servant in Miami which was Barker who later would play an important part in the Watergate burglaries.

Unfortunately for Hunt in the end, after his The Bay of Pigs operation was a disaster, Hunt along with the other creators in the Cuban Project found themselves in hot trouble in Kennedy administration. Kennedy administration. The CIA maintained Hunt employed, however in roles where Hunt was not a an active participant.

His first post-Bay Of Pigs job was that of as the Chief of Covert Action for the DOD (Domestic Operations Division) which is the division that is responsible for manipulating the media and conducting internal surveillance over American citizens. As these operations came to light the CIA was dragged onto the stage in the Rockefeller Commission in 1975.

In 1964 in 1964, the Agency appeared to have lost its enthusiasm on Hunt. The is the year in which CIA director John McCone permitted Hunt to move to Madrid in order to concentrate on writing the James Bond-style novels featuring a protagonist who was a communist, Peter Ward, who also was adept at disguise. A few years later, Hunt and his family returned to the States and bought the estate located in Potomac, Maryland known as Witches Island. Hunt returned to work at DOD and continued to work for the division until he retired in the CIA on April 30, 1970.

The CIA was able to help Hunt to get a job with Mullen & Company, a small PR company that could also be an official front to the CIA. Hunt was hired as a journalist for the company but found the work environment a bit stifling. Although he was earning an annual salary of $24,000 and was receiving an annual salary of $20,000 from the CIA but the cash flow was a bit tight. The mortgage and maintenance on the Witches Island estate was considerable as well as three and half years prior, Hunt's daughters had been involved in an automobile accident that resulted in significant medical expenses. The oldest daughter was afflicted with brain injury and was hospitalized in a medical facility within Maryland up to the point that Hunts were unable to be able to afford her stay there. According to Hunt's autobiography that he was even borrowing money from CIA Director Richard Helms.

At this point, Hunt had already met Charles (Chuck) Colson and was another fellow Brown University alumnus. Colson was Counselor to the White House Counsel and was determined to get his President elected in the next year. The most threatening issue was recent leaks to the media of confidential information notably known as the Pentagon Papers Daniel Ellsberg had given the to The New York Times. To stop the leaked information, Colson created a special investigative team consisting of "plumbers," and in July, he hired Hunt as well as ex- FBI agents G. Gordon Liddy to join the team.

In the case of Hunt this was an hourly work and he had to take a cut in his salary to get the job. (In the course of an interview William F. Buckley, Hunt said he earned only half of what he made for his job at Mullen.) The job also included an office at the White House, and the ever-expanding Hunt was hoping to turn this job into something much more important.

The initial couple of months of his responsibilities included travelling across Rhode Island to interview a source who claimed to have damaging information regarding possible Presidential candidates Ted Kennedy, an operation which resulted in Hunt to acquire disguise materials from old acquaintances at the CIA: a wig fake glasses, and a voice altering device. Then , in the month of September Hunt as well as Liddy planned an attempt to break into Daniel Ellsberg's psychiatrist's office to find evidence that could challenge Ellsberg's motives behind leaks of damaging information. The plan included traveling to California to investigate the doctor's office, and enlisting three Cuban American accomplices--among them Bernie Barker. Then, they flew the trio to Miami in the direction of California to complete the dirty job. Naturally, as an adrenalin addict, Hunt wanted to perform the burglary by himself, however Bud Krogh, his boss, resisted the idea which left Hunt to beg for mercy the fact that he was now an actor in the back of his chair.

They picked for the Labor Day weekend to execute the plan, hoping that the doctor would be off on vacation. While the group was able to break into the office and managed to escape without being arrested, nothing of value was discovered. However, the task itself was a good way to reinvigorate Hunt. He even celebrated the moment with champagne.

Following week while back to Washington, Hunt met with an agent from the CIA for lunch. Hunt was looking to settle the issue with his annuity and wanted to alter the terms of the contract so that his wife could be designated survivors. According to an CIA memo that was issued, when Hunt was told that the Agency denied Hunt's request, Hunt threatened to contact his fellow members of the White House.

A week later, on the advice of Colson, Hunt fabricated a series of telegrams that made it appear as if the Kennedy administration was at the forefront of the killing plot of South

Vietnamese president Ngo Dinh Diem. Hunt attempted unsuccessfully to present the cables as genuine to the Life Magazine reporter.

Except for the Christmas party hosted by Nixon and his family, following the Diem incident, Hunt's location is mostly unknown until January, after which Hunt together with G. Gordon Liddy began creating what would become known as Operation Gemstone, an attempt to create chaos at the forthcoming Democratic National Convention. Liddy claims in his memoir that Hunt was on a trip to California and Miami conducting preliminary work to support the Nixon campaign in this time however, Hunt states that the travels didn't happen until the beginning of the year.

What Hunt did in the final month of 1971 is unrecorded, however on the 7th of January of the next year Hunt purchased the Mexico tourists pass to Mexico for three months under his name as Edward Hamilton, one of the names that Hunt used during his time in the CIA. In the same time, John Mitchell released the Cooper serial numbers to the public. Two months later John Mitchell would step down as Attorney General and would take over the Nixon campaign for reelection and become the chief of staff of Hunt and began serving for his campaign around the same as.

The same month, one of the most bizarre tales of Hunt was uncovered. In the year prior an email composed by Republican campaign contributor Dita Beard came to light revealing an association between a gift Beard made and an antitrust favorable decision. The intention was to convince Beard to dismiss the memo as fraud, Charles Colson instructed Hunt to travel into Colorado to visit an ailing Beard in identical brown hair that he'd been wearing when he interviewed an anti-Kennedy source at Rhode Island. Hunt then tried to intimidate the weak Beard to agree to join his Nixon administration, but to but no result.

The next few months were dedicated to aiding G. Gordon Liddy launder some of the campaign funds Nixon was receiving, as well as performing preliminary work to prepare for Operation Gemstone, which involved trips to California and Miami.

On May 28, Memorial Day weekend, Hunt's burglars' team comprising Jim McCord and four Cubans who had travelled from Miami tried to gain entry into the headquarters of the Democratic National committee in the Watergate Hotel, ostensibly to intercept the phone number of the chairman of the committee, Larry O'Brien. The attempt failed (the burglars weren't able to open the door's lock) and so did the following, and the third attempt to break in was launched on the 17th of June. The thieves were caught by a vigilant security guard and two police officers who were undercover. As Hunt's child St. John, the day following the Watergate burglary, Hunt took St. John to the local bank which is where he drained a huge amount of cash from the safe deposit box. (Bank documents confirm that Hunt took some items from the safe deposit container on that date.) This cache was later hidden inside an air vent near his home. St. John estimated the value of the stash at somewhere between $300,000 and $100,000. After that, when Hunt's number was discovered in a Cuban's addresses The FBI began searching for Hunt and hoped to interrogate Hunt. Instead of turning himself into the police, Hunt disappeared for a week, before turning up at the residence of a lawyer friend, Morton "Tony" Jackson in Beverly Hills.

Then, in September of 1972 Hunt along with the others on his group were arrested. They were all detained to be tried or be sentenced. The time was when Hunt tried to intimidate to the Nixon administration, by threatening to expose potentially damaging secrets without payment to him and the families of others on the team. In a letter addressed to the administration, he set his deadline for November 25, which happened to be the weekend which coincided with the anniversary of one year of the Cooper skyjacking.

At this point in the course of his career, Hunt already had a number of prerequisites that make Hunt an ideal D.B. Cooper candidate. He had completed training in survival in the wilderness and parachute jumping within the OSS. He was taught skills that were clandestine and had planned and executed secret missions in the CIA. He'd written numerous spy fictions, displaying the power of imagination as well as an ambition to lead a James Bond life style. He had been a participant in classified CIA operations, such as those of the Air America campaign, which made use of Boeing 727s to drop items into foreign territory. He'd donned disguises for three missions. He'd developed a criminal history by committing two burglaries that were well-known. He'd been known to be adept at performing a plethora of operations during holiday weekends (Labor Day 1971, and Memorial Day, 1972). He'd amassed between $300,000 and $100,000 over the span of 15 months. And , as we'll discover, he matched the physical description offered by the witnesses more than the other D.B. Cooper suspect to date.

The people who have studied the D.B. Cooper case may talk about something called"the Cooper Curse. It is believed that those who are involved in the case suffer unfortunate luck. Family members of the boy who discovered the $6,000 in Cooper cash was afflicted with numerous difficulties. Two stewardesses who stayed long hours with Cooper each went into a state of solitude. The man who packed the parachute Cooper utilized was killed by an unknown attacker. At the very least, a Cooper suspect has had his life turn upside down after being publicly accused of being the notorious outlaw.

In the event that we conclude that the most significant sufferer of Cooper's Cooper Curse will be Cooper the man himself, it's impossible to not notice how horrific Hunt's situation had become only a few months following the NORJAK theft. Hunt's identity as an CIA agent was questioned and his name was a part of news reports across the globe due to the incorrect motives. He was incarcerated in an D.C. prison, fired by his boss at Mullen & Company, and was thrown out by the CIA and his annuity had been canceled. Unfairly or not the CIA would take a lot part of the responsibility for Nixon's demise.

A much more tragic event took place two weeks to on the anniversary of the Cooper heist.

On the 8th of December the year 1972 Hunt's wife Dorothy passed away in an unintentional air crash after the aircraft which was carrying her crashed on the descent into suburban Chicago. It was partly due to the fact that Dorothy Hunt had on her $10,000 in $100 bills, in part due to the fact that she had an attache bag whose contents are still unknown, also due to the fact that she bought an additional ticket to the empty seat adjacent to hers, and partially due to the fact that the FBI came to the scene shortly after the crash. Numerous conspiracy theories have been proposed in order to explain the events that became known in the name of "the Watergate crash." The most common belief is that the cash Dorothy carried on her was intended to serve as an offer to pay off some of the families of Watergate burglars who desperately required money for the legal defence they needed. In the event, Hunt inadvertently sent his wife to the grave through a bungled Watergate break-in.

In the case of E. Howard Hunt, there was a bright side to the tragedy. Before she boarded her plane, Dorothy purchased a life insurance policy. After she died, Hunt came

into the possession of $250,000 from the insurance company.
Nearly the same amount D.B. Cooper took.

Chapter 5: The Many Faces Of D.B. Cooper

The first thing that a uninitiated observer might notice when looking through the D.B. Cooper investigation is the numerous sketches drawn from testimony of witnesses. Of the blunders the FBI committed during its forty-five years investigation, the most serious could have been the release of multiple sketches that were not released to the public. The sketches do not have a lot in common with each other, leading to conclude that the FBI had a motive to make the waters more murky in order to stop D.B. Cooper from being discovered or Cooper had a sophisticated method of mind control, which caused different witnesses to view Cooper differently. However, if one looks at the way and the time the sketches were created it is evident that only one sketch can be considered trustworthy, and the others should be rejected.

Which are the most reliable sketches and the reason for that?

The first step is to take a an examination of the witnesses that the FBI faced. Three stewardesses interacting with Cooper: Alice

Hancock and Florence Schaffner as well as Tina Mucklow. Hancock was the most senior flight attendant, however she had only a few minutes with Cooper. Schaffner was the Stewardess Cooper gave an ransom notice to. But after the ransom was paid, Schaffner handed the responsibility into Mucklow. It was Mucklow who was the one who spent the longest time with Cooper around five hours, with the four hours she sat with Cooper. Mucklow was also the final person to meet Cooper prior to his departure from the plane.

There were 36 passengers on the plane. Only one was seated Cooper's front. Cooper The only chance they had to see Cooper came when Cooper took off and walked by, or when the passengers made their way towards Cooper as they headed to the toilet on the plane. The passenger who was just across the aisle to Cooper is William Mitchell, a 20-year-old student at a college. After the pilots learned of the possibility that Cooper carried a bomb on board and the stewardesses shifted Mitchell along with the other passengers three rows ahead of Cooper. In no moment in the course of flight did Mitchell or any of the other passengers realize that the plane was taken over by a terrorist.

The only remaining ticket agent who offered Cooper tickets, Dennis Lysne. His memory was exceptional. He remembered Dan Cooper's name as well as general information about the man.

As the passengers departed from Seattle The first sketch, also called the "initial sketch"--was likely drawn by an FBI field agent. The sketch was based upon evidence provided by Robert Gregory, who was one of three witnesses to estimate Cooper's age as thirty-five. Other witnesses said that they had Cooper somewhere between the mid-forties to the early fifties. In contrast to others, Gregory also described Cooper's hair as black, slack and marcelled. Gregory also described Cooper's suit color was described as "reddish and brown" and his glasses were described as horn-rimmed.

Even with all this detail, or perhaps because of it, his description of Cooper is extremely suspicious. Cooper was not sitting directly across from Cooper and, according to his testimonies, was the last passenger on board, which means that Cooper did not pass by him while he was walking to his seat. Gregory also got some key details incorrect in his account before the FBI. Gregory claimed that the passengers weren't moved three rows before the plane arrived in Seattle and was wrong by two hours. He also claimed to have seen an "brown-haired" Stewardess next to Cooper on the plane, but actually, the stewardess that was sitting right next to Cooper (Tina Mucklow) had blonde hair that was light. According to his own account, Gregory only caught a few glimpses of Cooper when he sneaked in glances by turning from his seat. After reading through the FBI report and observing the bizarre details contained only in Gregory's testimony it's difficult not to think that Gregory would like to be an expert witness more than he actually was by embellishing his testimony somewhat. The initial sketch depicts Cooper in his early years. Cooper with a full hairline and attractive face. This sketch is so different of Cooper from the description of the witnesses that it's not surprising that the FBI immediately commissioned a fresh sketch to be created shortly after the initial Sketch was made public.

FBI Agent Roy Rose made most or all the sketches. Based on the account Rose delivered in the year 2011 shortly after the hijacking, he flew to the Northwest Orient's Airlines' corporate headquarters in Minnesota and had a meeting with the three Stewardesses. (The FBI files back this up with a memo from 11/26/71.) He based his subsequent Cooper sketch on the descriptions of his. It was dubbed"the" Bing Crosby sketch, because the character in the sketch is a little like the famous Crosby. In this rendition, Cooper is clearly middle-aged and has thin hair, with short-cropped locks parted on the left side; a wide broad forehead, with wide worries lines, a sloping mouth and a sagging jaw. Cooper's face appears to be almost unnoticeable However, he had at least one distinct characteristic that emerged during the procedure and that was a lower lip that was protruding or puckered, something the artist was not able to make clear to the delight of the stewardesses.

Since the three women stayed in the greatest amount time Cooper and were able to remember his facial features, and especially because the drawings were created within a few hours of the incident, this sketch should be thought to be the most reliable. After reading all the FBI report, it's clear that Mucklow particularly had an enthralling memory. She also remembered details such as the kind of shoes Cooper was wearing.

However...there was a small issue with the sketch. There were there were no eyes.

None of the stewardesses seen a clear view of the stewardesses. Cooper was wearing sunglasses for the majority of the flight, but only Schaffner got a chance to look into his eyes. She didn't remember anything regarding their form, however it was clear that the color of his eyes was brown. Therefore, the sketch created by cooperating Stewardesses show Cooper wearing sunglasses.

However, this photo of Cooper did not suffice. To capture the full Cooper's appearance The FBI then turned to passengers as witnesses and requested their opinion hoping that they thought of what Cooper's eyes were like. The feds also wanted to find out what the witnesses--including the stewardesses--thought of the sketch Rose had made from the stewardesses' testimony. The files that the FBI made available to the public are censored and hide witnesses' names which makes it difficult to tell who thought what.

To begin with, Tina Mucklow and Alice Hancock believed that the drawing was an accurate representation of the artist. One of them said that "it was close to exactly similar to Cooper" but they could not provide any additional details that would ensure that it was accurate. Florence Schaffner, on the contrary, believed that the drawing was not a good depiction of Cooper. For the other passengers, the majority of them agreed that Roy's sketch was similar to the image Cooper was like. What they believed needed adjustment to it was the size that Cooper's facial features. The majority thought that it was too thin. The chin may not have been quite rectangular. Many claimed that the skin flap hanging under Cooper's chin was not visible sufficiently on the drawing. Many agreed that the hairline was the correct one but a few witnesses suggested that the hairline needed to be lowered. With the help of a facial recognition device Two witnesses provided some guidance on the shape of the eyes and both opted for eyes with heavy lids. One of the witnesses commented that Cooper had average eyes "of a Latin appearance, with a sort of disinterested...let's-get-it-over-with look." Two witnesses thought the Bing Crosby sketch made Cooper look younger than he was. Two witnesses believed Cooper's nose was larger than the sketch.

Apart from adding eyes to the sketch that the stewardesses made together with Rose It doesn't seem that those suggestions of the passengers were taken into another Bing Crosby sketch. It makes sense considering how the stewardesses communicated with Cooper much more frequently than the other passengers and, without doubt, were more familiar with Cooper.

The FBI then took the two Bing Crosby sketches and distributed the sketches widely. The tips of concerned citizens pour into. One man even wrote to the FBI to inform them that a character who resembled Cooper from the Cooper sketches had appeared on an episode from the television series Perry Mason.

The tips given by the public appeared to be false leads which is why, after spending almost six months looking into 500 false leads, the FBI was becoming frustrated. The first thing to note is that the suspects they ended in pursuing were light-skinned, not olive-skinned or swarthy as certain witnesses claimed Cooper to be. The others were too young.

The FBI looked over the records of the case and published the memo on May 30, 1972, containing suggestions that they believed the Bureau could follow to enhance the investigation. The topic the memo focused on was the most relevant to sketches drawn by the FBI sketches. The memo statesthat "One important witness [specifically Florence Schaffnerwas extremely insistent in her claim that the concept of the artist wasn't a great replica to the person who hijacked. It is suggested that an Bureau artist be transported to relevant divisions, which include Minneapolis, Seattle, and Portland and spend the required time with witnesses to ensure that the sketch of an artist that is deemed acceptable by most of the witnesses is obtained."

Evidently, the FBI did not realize that two sketches had been accepted from the vast majority witnesses, namely sketches from Bing Crosby sketches.

In addition, the memo suggested the color selection guide could be utilized to include specifics not usually present in black and/or white sketches.

Three months had passed after which on August 4th, a memo was issued that made the same argument to draw a different sketch. The memo's creator offered more information about Florence Schaffner's concerns about the sketch before, stating that the facial expression Schaffner selected from a facial identification kit was actually identical in appearance to that of that of the Bing Crosby sketch. with the principal difference being that the model that was in Bing Crosby's sketch. Bing Crosby sketch was too young.

But, despite that particular fact and the general agreement among people who testified that Bing Crosby sketches were accurate representations of Cooper however, the FBI took the decision to begin over again, and consider Schaffner's testimony to be more credible than other testimony. Her endorsement of a sketch at the time seemed to be the sole thing to consider. According to Schaffner's initial choice from the kit for facial identification, the face's shape was altered from an oval shape to a more triangular design. Two days later, two more sketches were drawn. They were the first two "B" sketches. This sketch by Cooper is a much more sinister suspect. He has a shorter hairline (kind similar to Sean Connery's hairline in his Goldfinger period) and a larger nose, a more rounded jaw, eyes that are further apart as opposed to the earlier sketch and eyebrows that slant downwards in a frightening way.

In September of this year, ten months following the Cooper heist -- the FBI began showing the latest sketches to the witnesses in order to hear their opinions. One witness believed that the sketch was great, but he was of the opinion that the hairline was too low and also that the shade of the skin should be lighter.

The second witness believed that the features were correct, but wanted the skin to be darker.

There's no consensus.

The witness next to him objected to that "nasty" as well as "angry" style of the character in the sketch. They said to the fact that Cooper's "swarthy" appearance is believed to be the work of Cooper could be due to the plane's light sources.

A third witness to the incident thought that the subject looked old on the drawing.

After a couple of weeks, the sketch was shown by one of the Stewardesses likely Alice Hancock, who deemed the sketch "an outstanding resemblance" and an "definite enhancement" over the sketch before. However, in a reversal of her assessment she said that the B sketch appeared to be more of a "hoodlum" kind of design however this was not true. Cooper She said that Cooper had more finesse than what the sketch in the B sketch, and not as "tough and rough." In addition, as many witnesses to the incident have already said that she believed the nose was not correct, too wide. It was not as precise as the sketch that was first drawn. Like witnesses of the passengers she was dissatisfied with the lip shape in the sketch B.

We then come the case of Tina Mucklow, who was interviewed on the very same day Hancock. As opposed to the other witnesses Mucklow was honest and admitted that it had been so long since she was passed that her memory was blurred. She also said she only have seen Cooper's profile which is difficult to believe considering the amount of time she spent with Cooper. Maybe all this was done in order to make the sketcher feel better about the judgment that she would soon give in the end, which was that the sketch was, according to the FBI report-- "definitely not a great likeness to the unsub [unknown subject. The sketch artist felt that B wasn't 'him' and Cooper's face was completely lost in the sketch with no sunglasses. Particularly, she said that the hairline drawn on sketch B was not correct and she preferred the hairline of the original sketch." In actual fact she said that the original concept was more like Cooper as the sole thing which could make this Bing Crosby sketch more accurate was less hair that was wavy.

Unfortunately for the FBI its most trusted witness had just poured cold water over those B sketches.

It wasn't just her witness to believe that the first sketches of the B were a dud. On October 4, the FBI issued a memo stating that two witnesses informed that the FBI they believed the drawings "no more resemble" their perceptions of the unsub. They also said they weren't completely satisfied with the previous conception however they believed it was more to the new version." It's not a good thing.

However, even Florence Schaffner wasn't completely satisfied. She thought Cooper's eyes in a proper way however she felt that the hair on real Cooper was less thick and more like that of Cooper's Bing Crosby sketch. She wasn't convinced that the sketched mouth was quite as accurate. However, in the overall she felt that the sketch was an "fairly decent resemblance" of the hijacker, as one would expect since it was based on her earlier ideas.

The madness didn't stop with the initial sketch. Roy Rose then made another sketch based on the contradictory and sometimes confusing suggestions from witnesses. On November 21 the following year, almost a whole year following the Cooper heist, the new, Frankensteinian sketches were shown to two passenger witnesses. Both agreed with them, even though one witness commented that the character in the sketches was "too ugly and gruesome."

The sketches were presented at the hands of one of the officers likely Alice Hancock, who stated that it is an "excellent" similarity, but she felt that the nose shouldn't appear so "rough or sloppy," and the mouth should appear less youthful.

On December 1, Mucklow was shown the updated B sketches. She claimed that she had only seen Cooper's profile. In the end, she claimed that even though the new sketches were a step up over the previous sketch, the B drawings weren't an "vivid depiction of the look" that Cooper possessed. Cooper.

Evidently, that was sufficient to please the FBI. On the 4th of January 1973, the most recent sketches were widely distributed to media outlets, a late Christmas present to anyone was the actual D.B. Cooper was, as the final sketches could have were more like James Bond more than D.B. Cooper.

Strangely enough, it was not until a month later that the sketches of B were made available to the press that the FBI demanded Florence Schaffner to give her impression of the sketches as they were finalized, in case she was afraid to render a negative review and challenge the bureau's shoddy method of revisions to the sketches of witnesses. Luckily they got Schaffner's approval. endorsed these sketches and stated that even though the forehead wasn't perfect she considered "the drawing to represent a great representation of the person who was the perpetrator," and she was of the opinion that "the hijacker could easily be identifiable in the sketch."

In spite of their intentions, the FBI has just caused more confusion. What they didn't be aware of was that memories change and they can become corrupted with time. We know that the first memories of an event, by the top witnesses are the most trustworthy.

To add to the confusion during the year 1988 on the TV show Unsolved Mysteries, Florence Schaffner expressed doubt about the credibility of all the FBI sketches. She then sat down with a police art director to offer what she believed to be an accurate rendition. As you can see, the man that appears on sketch Unsolved Mysteries sketch looks little like the characters in sketches. He's got a bizarre widow's peak, a large mouth as well as a large nose and a high cheekbone.

Yet , despite this incoherent method of making an impression of Cooper when one studies the FBI reports immediately following the incident and then compare those reports along with Cooper's sketch Bing Crosby sketch, useful details emerge. If the same traits are observed by several witnesses, even in the event that they're not observed by any other witness--they are likely to be true.

Many witnesses, for instance, mentioned Cooper's dark-colored complexion. Some witnesses observed it to be olive, namely

Florence Schaffner as well as Alice Hancock. Some others described it as "swarthy." Whatever Cooper is, it's evident that his skin tone was darker than usual.

However on the other hand, the only one Robert Gregory described Cooper's sunglasses as horn-rimmed and only Tina Mucklow saw them as wraparound. Others have described his glasses as brown-lensed. There isn't a consensus on the kind of sunglasses Cooper was wearing, but there is no doubt that he was wearing sunglasses.

Greg Labissoniere (the other witness who estimated Cooper's age at 35) stated that Cooper was wearing Cooper was wearing a "sporty" shirt. Nobody else was able to see the vest.

Cord Harms Zrim Spreckel estimated Cooper's age at 50, and said Cooper had the square jawline.

The majority of witnesses have described Cooper as being of medium build however, the information about his height varied widely based upon the person's gender. The stewardesses described Cooper to be about 6 feet tall. (Only Alice Hancock put him at 6'1". ."). Robert Gregory, Cord Spreckel,

Greg Labissoniere, and William Mitchell all estimated his height at 5 9" or 5'10". Gregory declared that the height was "short."

If we look at these descriptions with the sketches of the stewardesses distinct characteristics are revealed:

Cooper was a woman with receding hairlines

Cooper had dark, thin curly hair, with a short cut and parted to the left

Cooper had a broad forehead

Cooper was clean-shaven.

Cooper's eyes were full of glares.

Cooper had a sagging chin

Cooper had an upper lip that protruded or puckered

Cooper was dark-colored. It could be olive-colored

It is also possible to infer certain things from the things that were not discussed. If something didn't be noticed or spotted in the eyes of the witnesses then we can assume it was normal.

Cooper did not have huge or protruding ears, nor ears that were unusually shaped.

Cooper didn't have a nose that was funny.

Cooper was not afflicted with an obvious cleft on his chin.

Cooper did not sport the bushy eyebrows of his peers or unibrows.

Cooper was not afflicted with visible marks or tattoos.

Cooper was not bald.

Cooper was not noticeably overweight.

The combination of the traits we're fairly certain Cooper had and those we're fairly certain that he didn't possess can help in identifying or validating the suspicion of a suspicious.

How do Hunt do to this comparison? Well, quite well. He was just turning 53 at the time that the NORJAK incident happened and he was fairly good health (according to his own account, that he exercised at an exercise facility) and, in the dimly illuminated inside the cabin of the plane, it was difficult to make a good read about his age.

As of the Bing Crosby sketch, during this time Hunt had growing hairline (identical to that in the drawing) with a swath on the left as well as a large forehead, visible worry lines, a downward-turned jaw, similar-shaped ears as well as a skin flap resting beneath his cheeks. Hunt also had a big jaw, although not necessarily square in shape.

His eyes were heavy with lids. In his photos, he usually shows a bored "let's finish it off" expression.

Google photos of Hunt and you'll not have a problem finding images of him sporting a the lower lip which occasionally extends when he's speaking. (This feature can also be seen in the interviews of Hunt from the 70s-era in YouTube.)

Height: 5'10 1/2, not wearing shoes According to one record in the CIA Personnel file. His passport from 1971 indicates that he stood 5 9".

For the skin it appears that in the majority of photos Hunt has a good tanning. However, there are some exceptions. of him during the Watergate hearings. However, at the time of Hunt's life Hunt had been imprisoned and sun was an uncommon luxury. But, no one would call his tan an olive hue. The color is more bronze. Nearly orange. It is possible that Hunt applied dark-colored makeup prior to taking off on the plane? Perhaps. It is certainly true that he used to conceal his face. However, this seems somewhat unlikely because it is likely that after putting the makeup on for a few days, that the oil that were present in the skin could have resulted in the makeup running across the surface. In addition, he'd need apply it on his hands too. Most likely, the witnesses would be able to see any areas where the makeup was fading.

Hunt's other features are--like Cooper's--nondescript. A biographer described them as "forgettable." Hunt's sole identifying features Hunt was known for (protruding the lower part of his lip a flap of skin beneath the chin and wide forehead, heavy eyelids the receding of the hairline) were all noted by witnesses.

If Hunt weren't really D.B. Cooper It appears increasingly to be like someone having a bizarre perception of humor would like people to believe it was.

Chapter 6: Cia So, Are You A Friend Or Foe?

After the first information was revealed after the D.B. Cooper Heist One of the more bizarre theories was revealed to explain the event: D.B. Cooper was an CIA agent in the middle of a black-ops. The appearance of Cooper was typical G-Man: clean cut with a dark suit and tie with a trench coat and sunglasses. Then there was the manner of speaking that was polite and direct talking, and the professional, cool way in which he conducted his business from start to finish. In reality, Cooper seemed more like a person who was trained by the Agency rather than a brutal criminal. (What is it that a thug is willing to pay for his drink before taking the plane and the passengers captive?) What better explanation for Cooper's disappearance than the fact that he had some help from his friends from the Agency?

For sober Cooper investigators, this suspicious theory was not given much weight until the world was informed about the Air America operation, which was backed by the CIA in Vietnam called Air America.

It was the Air America campaign was an innovative method of dropping weapons, supplies and agents into overseas territories with civilian aircraft, including Boeing 727 airliners. Why this particular model? It was because it had the distinctive feature of having an aft staircase that could be raised mid-flight. This allowed the plane to travel over hostile territory without raising suspicion or appearing to break treaties. It could also securely drop whatever cargo was wanted without needing to bring the plane down. The program was so successful that it was utilized from 1962 until 1975.

Whatever Cooper did, they certainly had knowledge of Air America. When he purchased his flight ticket in Portland Cooper made an effort to ask the clerk at the counter whether the plane he'd fly on was an Airbus 727 to make sure that it was the right model. He appeared to be confident in the process that jumping off an airplane during a flight was nothing to worry about. The less experienced bandits could have been worried about being caught in one of the engines trying to pull off such an act. In other plane models this was a possibility.

Cooper was also able to comprehend the precise procedures involved in dropping cargo from an aircraft. Cooper instructed pilots to fly under 10,000 feet, to reduce the cabin's pressure and to fly at the right speed by lowering the flaps. It wasn't the first time that he had prepared an aircraft 727 to drop things from the stairs in the rear.

Who would then have been in possession of Air America in 1971? The CIA clearly. Also, the civilian crew and pilots who were flying the missions during the time along with their Boeing engineers who had helped to design the airliner.

However, the FBI did not do anything to investigate Boeing engineers or Air America pilots, or Vietnam veterans They had forty-five years to do their homework.

The CIA was further questioned after reporter Geoffrey Gray discovered that during the initial search for Cooper's body, the SR-71 Blackbird spy plane, that is a plane that the CIA typically reserved in the event of surveillance operations, utilized to aid with the investigation. The existence of the plane is thought to be to be highly unusual.

Then the notions of Cooper being connected to the CIA did not seem as absurd.

However, the FBI did not seem to be keen to look into this Air America connection, which was discovered early into the inquiry. On the 7th of December, 1971, a sleuth-in-the-know wrote a letter in hand in the direction of Northwest Airlines' corporate office informing them of what he believed was an opportunity to discover Cooper's identity. The letter writer, two months prior to the Cooper theft, he was onboard the Northwest Airlines 727 en route to Seattle. He had an exchange with another passenger who claimed that he had flown "727s for military use dropping supplies and personnel in areas that were otherwise unaccessible." He stated that he too had been a jumper from 727s during the course and that it was "a thrilling experience." After concluding that the plane was traveling somewhere in Asia The letter writer concluded that the pilot was piloting the planes of the CIA and he was able to conclude that Cooper was connected in the Agency.

A Northwest Airlines executive who received the letter stated that the theory was "far out" however, he passed it to FBI nevertheless.

Waiting for the FBI to get in touch with the writer of the letter, he followed up with a letter on the 12th of December, laying out the evidence for his hypothesis and this time, to his senator Henry A. Jackson. The letter urged senator Jackson to inquire with the CIA to find out if they'd been instructing pilots on how to drop supplies into inaccessible areas, and, if so what percentage of those pilots were able to return back to normal life (assuming they could include Cooper). The letter writer later revealed that he'd taken the initiative to look into the issue, and contacted Boeing to inquire if any of their aircrafts might be used by the military to carry out similar missions to those the unidentified passenger was referring to. A Boeing agent he spoke to replied in the negative, telling him that "there isn't one single 727 aircraft in the inventory of military aircraft. There's been no military pilot who has been trained in a 727. Nor have they ever been utilized in jump schools. In fact, there hasn't been a written flight manual for the procedure of setting flaps to jumps. If the military ever utilized such a software, we'd have an erupting headline and a whole page with photos."

The answer seemed to satisfy the writer of the letter that the 727s were part the CIA program, not a military program.

The senator's letter appears to have caught the FBI's interest. On the 27th of December FBI agents made a trip to the letter's writer to discuss the incident. During the interview, the writer reiterated his belief that the person he'd met on the 727 had been piloted by seventy-nine planes with the CIA across Southeastern Asia, and that Cooper may be one of the pilots, or had gotten information about how to jump off the 727 from one of the pilots. He also said that "If due to the hijacking, we could discover this was a deliberate act by the CIA it could be the most serious mistake that has occurred since that U2 incident." He continued to suggest that no one would be able to determine the cause investigation into Cooper's story until after the Cooper incident until the next conference of the President Nixon in China in the fear of embarrassing the Nixon administration.

A fascinating theory, indeed.

For the letter writer in the course of the meeting with the FBI they discovered that the letter he wrote in the past was to "Communist newspaper." Then the FBI discovered many references to security probes into the past of the man, probably at the FBI headquarters in Seattle. Perhaps due to the fact that they doubted the motives of the man, there's no evidence that the agents investigated the information that he'd provided them.

The reader of today might be sympathetic to the FBI in not taking the same path, but should one believe that the CIA had more important tasks to accomplish than hijacking aircrafts and steal money in the beginning of the 1970s If you want to take a look back to the history of the CIA and the activities it engaged in during the time could prove helpful.

The Central Intelligence was established in 1947. the main purpose of the Central Intelligence was to collect intelligence generally from abroad on those who might be able to cause us harm. However, unlike their rivals the FBI the Central Intelligence was not established as a law enforcement organization. Their primary function was to maintain a shady watch on Cold War adversaries, especially the Soviet Union and China, as well as any other nation that was foolish enough to accept Communism or to get into opposition to American corporate interests.

The seemingly innocent purpose was not to last for very long. When Alan Dulles became head of the CIA in the year 2000, this Agency was more intent on trying to undermine governments run by Communist leadership, and this was done both in a subtle manner as well as sometimes more violently. One of the main components of their strategy was disseminating anti-communist propaganda in the hope that the citizens of the nation concerned would come out and oppose the notion of

Communism or accept Capitalism as well as the West or both.

The state-led organisations of today try to achieve the same goal by trying to control social media. As an example, Russians tried to influence the presidential election in 2016 Presidential election through the creation of Facebook accounts that would distribute anti-Clinton messages It was exactly the type of thing that Americans did in the Cold War against their communist opponents, only using the use of a different set. The simplest and simplest method of getting the attention of the public was to drop leaflets on people to take a look at. However, over time the CIA gained more funds and became more aggressive and discovered methods to communicate the message. It even went further than setting publishing companies in countries that were hostile to the West to put out books that were favorable towards Capitalism in the West from within. (In the the 1960s Hunt had been heavily involved with these kinds of operations.)

As the CIA expanded in power and size and power, it went on and more aggressive in its efforts to take down dictators whom who the American government thought were threat. In 1953, the Agency introduced MKUltra, a mind-control program which involved the administration of hallucinogens to unaware victims. The experiment continued until the beginning of the 1970s.

In the years following Fidel Castro became the president in the 1980s, The Eisenhower-backed Cuban Project, also known as Operation Mongoose, called for the CIA to launch a public relations program to defy the Castro regime and to create an army-like paramilitary organization to lead and train resistance groups against the same foe. Operation Mongoose led to the Bay of Pigs fiasco, that included CIA agents forming a coalition of Cuban exiles to take on Cuba and try to wrest control of the country away from Castro. Castro regime. (Hunt was among the key architects of the operation.)

After this operation failed it was followed by a furious CIA tried out more innovative strategies to thwart Communism like attempting to destroy Castro's scuba regulator device by introducing tuberculosis bacteria, and then serving the victim a poisoned ice cream, and lacing his cigars with a poison which would cause him to lose consciousness at the wrong moment and using a chemical to make his beard slide out and bribing mafia members to disarm from the Cuban leader. The CIA points for their creativity.

Another CIA famous program is Operation Midnight Climax, a program that was designed to gather information from subjects who were not aware of it by luring them to secure homes used by prostitutes, taking them under the influence of drugs and bribing them into submission.

Things were then pushed up by the introduction of Operation Chaos, a Nixon-era program that went well beyond the purpose of snooping on foreign threats and instead questioned Americans at home. To search out dissidents, the mail was often inspected for evidence of suspects and attempts were made to target suspected students on campuses. These types of activities were way beyond the agency's jurisdiction and were certainly not legal. It's important to keep in mind that Hunt was employed at the time and was active in certain operations.

It was followed by Operation Mockingbird, which didn't fully surface until 1977. In response to Soviet Union's manipulation of news media in Europe and the United States, the CIA established relationships with a variety of friendly American news agencies, convincing them to publish pro-West news stories created by the CIA and placing certain numbers of American journalists on their payroll. They also funneled information to them to ensure that only legitimate journalists could actually write the pro-West news articles.

Let's not overlook Swan Island, another key part of this anticommunist campaign. It is actually a group of islands located a few hundred miles from on the shores of Honduras It was initially utilized for the United Fruit Company to better manage the trade in fruits among Latin America and the United States. Then, the CIA was able to acquire the territory and in early 1950s , they began making use of the islands to transmit radio broadcasts in order to send anti-communist propaganda. Naturally, this kind of tactic was not new. The Japanese did something similar in the Tokyo Rose broadcasts during World War II However, the CIA went to a new level, accelerating the broadcast so that normal radio waves were able to reach all up to Cuba. Professional-sounding radio shows were recorded in Miami, then broadcast from Swan Island, though before long Castro jammed the radio waves so that the CIA's channel had little lasting impact. A few years after the radio war ended the truth was made clear that Hunt himself had come up with the idea while trying to get rid of Jacobo Arbenz from Guatemala.

All of these dubious programs did not compare with Operation Northwoods, a plan created in the year 1962 by the efforts of CIA together with the Joint Chiefs of Staff. Though never implemented--President Kennedy put the kibosh on it--it's interesting to learn just what lengths the CIA was willing to go to to thwart Communism. After the Bay of Pigs operation, the military wanted to enter a formal battle with Cuba. For both sides, Cuba was adamantly refusing to incite Americans to fight as the military devised an idea to come up with the "remember Maine" Maine" kind of act, by engaging in acts in opposition to Americans as well as American interests, while blame this on Castro. Castro Regime. The proposed actions included the use of plastic explosives to explode American targets shooting down fake American aircraft, orchestrating terror within U.S. cities, assassinating Cuban refugees and hijacking American airliners to fly the aircraft to Cuba. Are they hijacking American airliners? This is a ringing bell Isn't it?

One question that is needed to be addressed is: Was Hunt an active participant in the design and execution Operation Northwoods?

Well, perhaps. The person who demanded the actions that could mobilize people American people was General Brigadier Edward Lansdale, an old acquaintance of Hunt's dating back into World War II. When the idea was first thought in the first place, Hunt was working for DOD and it's not a big idea to think that Lansdale may have demanded Hunt to come with ideas. In his autobiography American Spy, Hunt mentions having a meeting the two with Lansdale as well as CIA director Richard Helms just after the Bay of Pigs and filling them in on the events that was wrong. Everything else they discussed remains a mystery to the past, however, Hunt states that in 1971when he was working at the White House, he interviewed Lansdale in Hunt's office, and in secret, he recorded their conversation. The conversation, too, has been lost to history, however, it's interesting that it happened in the weeks following the D.B. Cooper skyjacking.

In 1975, these suspect CIA operations were discovered in 1975 when the Senate created the Church Committee to investigate suspected of abuses committed from the Agency. The reason for this was due to the fact that many were concerned that the CIA may have been behind the Watergate burglaries, primarily because the team that was involved comprised the two ex- CIA agents, and at least one person who was placed on CIA payroll. In a way Hunt's blunders during the Watergate burglary resulted in Congress stopping CIA violations.

However, if that the CIA played a part with respect to cooper's execution Cooper hijacking, it's hard to think about what the motives could be. Most likely, it was Stopping skyjackings.

With our security screenings at airports post-911 we often forget how inflexible airports were in the past in terms of security. Prior to the 1960s it wasn't a huge problem, but when Congress introduced the travel ban for American flights to Cuba there was a surge of skyjackings began to occur in the United States and many flights transferred to Cuba. In 1971, more than 80 flights were hijacked and flown to Cuba. October was the only month that witnessed four hijackings that, in the end, resulted in deaths of flight attendants. Naturally, the best option was for airlines to install metal detectors as well as X-ray machines and begin screening passengers' luggage However, the airlines were hesitant to adopt this option due to the additional cost and concern that their passengers would dislike having their luggage checked through. Then there was the issue of whether searching passengers and their luggage without a warrant for search was in contravention of the constitution's Fourth Amendment.

The same reason--along with the worry about losing campaign contributions from airlines--neither Congress or the Nixon administration were too eager to impose regulations on airlines to do things right.

However, as it was the CIA was concerned, the constant skyjackings of Cuba were a public relations nightmare. Every incident became newsworthy and served to remind people that certain American citizens would rather reside in Cuba instead of the USA. Therefore, if the CIA was looking to stop the terror attacks to Cuba by requiring airlines to increase security, putting a man aboard an airplane carrying a bomb is an ideal way to begin. The fallout of the Cooper incident was predictable: There were scores of Cooper replicators smuggled weapons into planes, hoping to duplicate Cooper's accomplishment. They failed. Then, in February of 1972 a mere months after Cooper's theft, the FAA required that airlines check every passenger. More stringent regulations were enacted in

December of the same year. The hijackings ended.

Mission completed.

What does all that has to do with Hunt? anything to do with Hunt? The month of April was the year that Hunt quit the CIA. CIA. There's no doubt that Hunt was not in the CIA payroll at the time that Cooper Heist took place. Cooper Heist took place, which means that even if CIA was planning to carry out the same type of false-flag operation as the one described by Operation Northwoods, Hunt wouldn't have been involved, wouldn't he?

But not always but if the CIA wanted to carry out such a plan they could hire an unrelated contractor. If they had kept journalists on their payroll to aid in their propaganda campaigns, so why not contract out the most prominent hijacking incident to an employee who was previously employed?

There's a chance that Hunt did the operation with the knowledge or consent of the CIA If he were to be arrested and convicted, it's likely that the CIA would find his actions so embarrassing that they'd have to bail Hunt out and give an explanation of the incident as it was a test to check security measures at airports.

No matter if the CIA had knowledge of the operation beforehand regardless of whether they knew about the operation in advance, the Agency was likely to have been delighted that Cooper brought attention to what it considered to be a vulnerability within national security. It is likely that the Agency would have been more likely to aid an old brother in the event that Cooper was one of the victims. At this time, Hunt did in fact seek out the CIA to seek assistance. While on the trip to talk to Clifton De Motte in Rhode Island and was provided with masks. This was also true when the pair Liddy traveled to California to confront the Dr. Fielding's workplace. The Agency also supplied a surveillance camera as well as fake IDs. In January, as Liddy was working on for his Operation Gemstone presentation for John Mitchell The Agency assisted Liddy create the visual aids he needed.

Of course, if CIA truly were behind the Cooper scheme to encourage copycats and create air travel an absolute nightmare for airlines, Cooper had to get free of the charge. No one would be likely to be inspired by his actions when he was caught and thrown in the jail. For this particular method to prove successful, Cooper couldn't get caught.

Maybe the CIA might have some secrets to reveal, but if they do they're not revealing. The author submitted a FOIA request to obtain any information that they might give regarding their involvement with Cooper's hijacking. Cooper hijacking. They were not willing to divulge any information, or confirm or deny the existence of any relevant information--citing national security issues.

Sometimes, one must read in the midst of the text. Prior to when the Church Committee hearings began, the House of Representatives Armed Services Committee conducted a hearing at possible involvement of The CIA during Watergate. On June 28 in 1973, Hunt was hauled before the committee and interrogated to ninety minutes. While he was mostly quizzed about his involvement in Nixon's administration, Nixon Administration, however at some moment during a discussion between Hunt and the committee's chairman, congressman Lucien Nedzi, the questioning changed to a famous hijacking of an airliner. It's not the NORJAK case However, the question was related:

Nedzi Do you know anyone who goes by the name of George Ames, Mr. Hunt?

Hunt: Is it an actual name or a pseudonym? I can't think of a name. I'll give you straight off my head "No."

Nedzi when you worked for a time in Central America, did you ever have the opportunity to be in contact with those involved in electronically-based installation agreements in Guatemala or anywhere other than Central America?

Hunt: I might have. I'm not able to think of any. I was part of an operation called "Overthrow Arbens" in Guatemala You know. We utilized the subsidiary [deleted] as a component of our communication network. If you can give more specific details, please do so. This is the only connection I can come up with Sir. Also, I'm not familiar with the names of anyone else in the past.

Nedzi: Do know anyone who is or Frederick William Hahneman?

Hunt: Hahneman?
Nedzi: Yes, H-a-h-n-e-m-a-n.
Hunt: No, sir. To my best memory.
Nedzi:. Do you have any information about the May 5 1972, hijacking that took place on the Eastern Airlines flight from Allentown, Pa., to Washington and then Miami?
Mr. Hunt: No, sir.
The questioning line seems odd given that it is directly following Nedzi has inquired about whether Hunt's wife had removed any contents from his safe either at his White House Office or from his office at Mullen & Company following Hunt's arrest in connection with his role in the Watergate break-in. Frederick Hahneman was one of the most famous of the hijackers who imitated D.B. Cooper's heist. On May 5 1972, under his pseudonym George Ames, Honduran native Frederick Hahneman hijacked a Boeing 727 plane in Pennsylvania and then landed at Virginia's Dulles Airport, extorted $300,000 from an airline firm He demanded a parachutist to himself and then

ordered the plane to Honduras where it dropped.

Hahneman could have been one of one of the most violent Cooper copies. Instead of making use of his social skills to control his flight attendants, Hahneman smuggled a pistol onto the plane and then threw it at the stomach of any person who caused problems for him. In Dulles the crew had to change planes because of an issue with the mechanical system in the plane that he landed in and, when Hahneman led his flight crew onto the new plane, he carried a rope on the captain's neck.

It didn't take too long for the FBI to determine his identity however, Hahneman fled to the Honduran jungle, securing help from the villagers. After approximately a month in hiding Hahneman surrendered for the FBI. In somewhat baffling circumstances the FBI was able to recover all the loot stolen.

The most obvious question is: If Congress wanted to establish whether or whether it was the CIA is behind the break-ins in Watergate as well as Dr. Fielding's Office, why did they mention any of these D.B.

Cooper copycat hijackings? Maybe they thought the CIA could be involved in this incident If one considers the possibility, it's likely that the CIA could also be involved in the Cooper Heist.

In reality the Cooper theft and the Hahneman caper shared a interesting feature in both: They were perpetrated by men who was well into middle age. Cooper as well as Hahneman were both in their mid-forties or more. To give you an idea of the extent of their astonishment here is a list of the ages of skyjackers, whose plans were similar as Cooper's and were executed in 1971 or 1972. This includes Paul Cini, who committed his act 11 days prior to Cooper.

"Lomas" Unknown
Francis Goodell: 21
Everett Holt: 22
Billy Hurst: 22
Robb Heady Robb Heady
Richard Lapoint: 23
Daniel Bernard Carre: 25
Paul Joseph Cini: 26
Martin McNally: 28
Richard McCoy: 29
Stanley Speck: 31

Melvin Fisher: 49
Frederick Hahneman: 49

Skyjacking was, according to reports, an activity played by young men.

Apart from Cooper and Hahneman Only Melvin Fisher was older than 31 and Fisher decided to give up his life to avoid making the leap. Perhaps due to the fact that those Cooper as well as Hahneman cases were unusual for the age of the skyjacker, members of Congress believed they had evidence that the CIA was behind them both.

The more obscure question is: why was an elected official asking Hunt about the possibility of a Cooper copycat? Even If Congress was aware that they were aware that the CIA had been responsible for this Hahneman hijacking, how could they have believed Hunt to have knowledge of the incident?

Did there ever exist rumors of Hunt had been D.B. Cooper?

Another question that needs to be answered What was the reason Hunt apparently not aware of Hahneman's skyjacking Hahneman skyjacking? Even if

Hunt had nothing to do with it and was not a resident or worker within the D.C. area, like Hunt, would have been involved in the tale. Hunt's curiosity could have been further stimulated due to the fact that Hahneman was the pilot of the plane that took him into Latin America, one of Hunt's favorite places to go. Because Hunt was being questioned about the incident just less than a year after the event and it is a bit odd that Hunt would claim to not know about the case in any way.

Chapter 7: Preparing For Boarding

"American authorities were reluctant to introduce radical changes to air security, despite the three hijackings that occurred in Jordan. President Nixon demanded the standard response to the threat of armed sky marshals on certain flights. The more aggressive methods, such as metal detectors and baggage inspection were dismissed as unfit for air travel business. They could cause passengers nervous.

In the midst of that, Dan Cooper was able to travel unhindered on Flight 305 with a bomb--or what he claimed to be an explosive device, even when everyone in the travel industry was aware that the absence of security meant that any passenger could be able to take flight." -- Richard Krajicek, CrimeLibrary.com

On the 24th of November 1971 Cooper began to plan to move his idea in motion. He had picked the right date since airlines would be extremely overwhelmed and distracted from the countless passengers returning home to celebrate the holiday. When he woke up in the morning, he wore the black suit and carefully pressed white shirt and a black, somber tie, which was clipped by the mother-of pearl tie pin to secure it. He put a bottle Benzedrine pills into his pocket to make sure the group had issues staying awake. Then, the polished loafers were paired with an all-black raincoat. He also put two dark sunglasses into his pockets. In the end, Cooper was portraying an image that implied there no special qualities about him. However, it was his conservative business image that caught the eye of an airline employee at least as by 1971, male fashions were changing and patterns and color were the norm of the hour. Hal Williams would later tell the FBI, "Yes, as the truth is there was a gentleman who looked suspicious." But the FBI agent Himmelsbach stated, "He was your typical businessman wearing dressed in a suit, tie with a raincoat and an attache bag. He was not distinctive other than perhaps the appearance of everything dark, black tie black shoes, a black raincoat. Cooper was at the counter for tickets, purchased his ticket , and then said "I'm Cooper." Cooper."

The tie Cooper was wearing in the time of hijacking.

Cooper likely took a taxi to the airport as there was no vehicle that was connected to Cooper was ever discovered. Dennis Lysne, who was in charge of the ticket counter on the ticket desk at Portland International Airport that afternoon was already working all day. It was the mid-afternoon of the day that was Thanksgiving Day which is among the biggest day of flying in the year. From the moment he stepped on duty, he'd been bombarded with all kinds of questions. Lysne had to handle elderly women who wanted to know whether it was really appropriate to travel, mothers with young children worried about how their infants would react to pressure changes in the cabin, as well as people who were anxious about having the connection.

Cooper met Lysne just before the plane was set to take off . He requested, "Can I get on the flight you're taking for Seattle?" Cooper then asked Lysne, "That's a 727 that's not that?" After that was confirmed, Cooper paid for his $20 flight in cash. Lysne thought Cooper had missed something could have been caught when it was a quieter time, and the person who was referred to as "Dan

Cooper" appeared to be a normal hustler looking for the flight in time for the holidays. He wasn't in any way tall, at the very least for a man, and neither was he large or menacing or intimidating in any manner. He was wearing comfortable loafers and a black raincoat an everyday occurrence for those who lives or works in Seattle. His mother-of-pearl tie-pin was clean and shiny, as was his attache case was black and was fresh and may be fresh. It did not seem to Lysne as strange that Cooper only required a single ticket one way, and especially the flight between Portland to Seattle that was so small to have any importance.

After purchasing his ticket, Cooper was able to walk over to the area where he waited, and as other passengers waiting to take off on Flight 305 chatted in a small group, Cooper stood on his own. When it was his turn to take off on the Boeing 727-100 with only around three dozen passengers and therefore was mostly empty Cooper was seated in seat 18C towards the rear of the plane and settled down. He set his attache case on the seat beside him and lit a cigarette, which was the norm on airplanes in the early '70s. He requested the stewardess Florence Schaffner to give him a bottle of bourbon and 7 Up. When she informed him that it would cost him one dollar, he gave his $20 to her and informed her that it was the smallest amount that he'd ever had. She accepted the huge bill and said she would give him a change when she helped all the passengers.

Chapter 8: In The Air To Seattle

"The Two flight attendants that stayed the longest time in the aircraft were questioned on the same night in different cities and gave almost identical descriptions. Both said they were 5'10" to 6' 170-180 pounds, and was in his 40s and had brown eyes. People who had the contact of him provided identical descriptions." The Special Agent Larry Carr

"He wasn't nervous. He appeared to be quite charming. He did not seem cruel or rude. He was calm and thoughtful every moment of the day." - Flight Attendant Tina Mucklow

It took off according to schedule at around 2:50 p.m. It was shortly after the plane was in plane, Schaffner was walking past Cooper when she was handed an envelope. Thinking it was nothing like the norm the note was largely ignored by her the note while she threw the note in her purse. Cooper did not realize that she received love notes from passengers almost every day and to the point that she even took to wearing a wig to work. was working. So she assumed that Cooper was the one who gave her his phone number, and was not likely to bother to look it up right now.

Florence Schaffner

As the note was the initial step in his plan Cooper was required to draw her attention. So he told her, "Miss, you'd better examine that note. I've got an explosive device." Schaffner cut open the envelope and took out the heavy stationary. The letter was neatly written using all capital letters, using an ebony tip pen the letter read "I have an explosive inside my briefcase. I'll use it in the event of need. I would like you to sit right next to me. It's a prank." She glanced at Cooper who was staring at her in awe with no fear or urgency. She then believed it was a joke. Anyone who had any knowledge of the business knew that hijackers were typically terrorists or political refugees rather than businessmen dressed in a nice way who were drinking bourbon and 7-Up.

"You're kidding, aren't you?" she asked.

"No, miss. This is real."

Schaffner was seated in the vacant seat right next to him, exactly like he wanted. In the hope that it was something else than a joke, she wanted to look at the bomb, and

Cooper removed the attachment case only to reveal his invention. What Schaffner discovered was a gadget that appeared to have a battery, and cylinders that were attached to wires. The look of terror in her eyes, the man strode the copper wire , as to detonate it at the same time. Later, she recalled "I observed a large battery that had six dynamite sticks encased in the middle of it. He said to me, 'All that I have to do is to connect the wire to this device and then we'll die.'" Himmelsbach later speculated that Cooper developed the concept for the bomb after watching the famous film Airport that came out in the year before.

The flight was just 30 minutes, so Cooper was required to keep the plane going. When he put off his glasses He sat down and told Schaffner, "Take this down." After grabbing the pen out of bag, she wrote note of the following: "I want two hundred thousand dollars by five p.m. In cash. Keep it in a bag. I'd like to have two parachutes for the back and two parachutes in front. If we do land in the air, I'd like a fuel truck that is ready to refill. Nothing funny or snarky, I'll take care of it. There's no fuss. Then we'll go on an excursion." But when Schaffner informed him that she needed to bring this note back to the cabin, he turned concerned, possibly due to the fact that he wanted her remain near him, or at the very least at a place where it was possible to monitor her. However the captain had to take this note in the hands of the Captain. Another stewardess Tina Mucklow, offered to take the note however he wasn't sure if he could trust her.

When Schaffner once more insisted she needed to get into the cockpit area, he accepted this time and said, "All right. Let's go." Schaffner later remembered the thoughts she had when she told that the crew sitting in the cockpit "We were all very terrified to death. We were all scared to death. I was thinking about my death. This is all I was thinking about. I also thought that I'll never meet my parents, sisters and brothers." In a couple of minutes after captain William Scott radioed Northwest Flight Operations across the nation from Minnesota: "Passenger has advised that this was an attempt to hijack. The plane is on its way to Seattle. The stew was handed an email. He wants the sum of $200,000 to be stuffed into a knapsack by 5 pm. He would like two parachutes from the back, and 2 front parachutes. He would like the money to be in the form of negotiable American currency. The denomination of the bills is not critical. A bomb is in the briefcase and is used if something is done to stop this request."

Tina Mucklow

Captain William Scott

After the authorities in the field were notified after which it was the responsibility of the airlines if they were willing to be able to pay for the ransom. Himmelsbach said, "The FBI asked the airline what their response to the hijacking might be, which is to say whether they wanted to make a payment for the ransom. This is a choice the victim of extortion can choose as opposed to law enforcement and they immediately responded that they wanted to settle the ransom. So the FBI in Seattle began to assist in obtaining the ransom."

While Schaffner was absent, Mucklow took her place next to Cooper when she returned. By it was time Schaffner came back, he was drinking another bourbon and 7-Up. When she delivered it before him, he quickly took out money and purchased the drinks. This was a bit of a shock to the stewardess, given his position in process of stealing the plane for $200,000. Noticing the expression of shock in her eyes, the man gave her with a smile of humour and instructed her to save the money. She asked him to tell her what he would like to see but he refused to reply, possibly trying to keep the plan in the dark for as long as it was possible.

Although he was aware of what he wanted, and was determined to obtain this, Cooper had nothing against Schaffner or any other person who was on the plane. In fact, he wanted to make the whole process as smooth as possible for all involved, and Cooper even considered it's possible that his plan could have the crew continue to eat their usual meal time. In this regard Schaffner was instructed to ensure that he ordered additional meals on the flight for the crew when they arrived in Seattle. There was no reason to be hungry.

The next question Cooper was interested in was whether passengers ought to be informed to the incident. Cooper probably had already thought about this issue, since he advised the pilot not to notify the passengers, but to think of a plausible explanation of the delays. Therefore, Scott got on the intercom and said calmly "Ladies ladies and gentlemen there's an unintentional mechanical issue. We've been instructed to go around Seattle in order to burn off excess fuel."

While he took a seat and enjoyed the second glass of wine It's hard to imagine what was going through Cooper's head as the pieces were getting in order at least so far. The captain did what was ordered and so had the stewardesses. The announcement signified that he wasn't required to worry about passengers. Although he may not know what activities were taking place between authorities and airline personnel at the ground level It is likely that he believed that his pilot would be constantly in communications with these people. It appears Cooper was concerned that radio signals could trigger the explosive or at the very least would like to make that clear and he instructed Mucklow to call the captain to express his concerns about radio signals. Scott was unsure whether the radio would cause the explosion to go off in any way, however he was aware that the need to remain on top of the ground. Moreover the messages he had sent out hadn't caused anything , so far.

In this moment the FBI was in the process of contacting the FBI and the following exchange was conducted:

Agent: "Do you know where the agent would like to head?"

Scott: "Negative. I've only asked him once, we're not going to repeat the question. I would suggest we put off the question and look at where he's willing to go."

Agent: "Can bring out the guides to Alaska If you believe that."

In the next few minutes the person inquired whether Cooper could hear radio signals. Scott responded, "I don't know. I believe you're free to call us. There's no problem for us up here. He's at the back."

Cooper was not just Cooper sitting in the back Cooper was having a blast on his flight more than the majority people in his group who were genuinely worried about the delayed landing. While they were worried about completing their next flight or getting off the ground in a safe manner Cooper was having a fling with Mucklow. As he pulled out a second cigarettes, he offered Mucklow a second one and, after she sipped the cigarette, they began an informal conversation. When Cooper inquired about where Mucklow was, Mucklow said that she was raised in an Philadelphia suburb, but is now located in Minneapolis. To this, Cooper replied, "Minneapolis is a very beautiful country."

Mucklow then tried to create an absurd joke that could be able to elicit information in the process. She said to Cooper, "You know Northwest Orient has strict guidelines against travel to Cuba. It is not allowed to bring back cigars or rum. Customs will confiscate them at the terminal." Cooper laughed and she replied, "No, we're not going to Cuba. But I think you'll enjoy the place we're headed to." At this point the discussion was disrupted by a tall man wearing a cowboy cap who wanted to know what was happening and the time they'd arrive. Because he could not comprehend the cowboy's confusion delighted Cooper however, when the hijacker got exhausted of the interruption, Cooper told him to return and sit down. He then looked over at Mucklow and threateningly told her, "If that's a sky marshal, I'm not interested in anymore of that." She swiftly assured Cooper "There no sky marshals on this flight 305." Happy, he went on to the next topic and told Mucklow to contact Schaffner and ask that she should bring the note to her, possibly since he didn't want the authorities to see any evidence that he wrote in his own hand.

As the two talked, Schaffner stopped by to inform Cooper that the business was working to put together the items he was looking for, such as parachutes they received from a military base in the area. Cooper protested because he was aware that military chutes were equipped with automatic opening mechanisms that give the jumpers no control over the length of time they would fall before they could deploy the canopy. He advised Schaffner to return to the cockpit to inform the captain in clear words that he needed civilian parachutes that had manual controls. In the end, the authorities needed to obtain parachutes from an civilian skydiving academy. The reason he asked for two parachutes also worried people on the ground since it appeared to suggest that he was planning to keep them as the hostage and cause them to jump. It is possible that authorities could give parachutes that actually performed, that's something Cooper might be thinking about when he made his request.

Then, Cooper returned to his conversation with Mucklow in which he made the comment that the airline was likely to have gotten parachutes directly from McChord Air Force Base, as it was located just 20 minutes away from the Seattle-Tacoma Airport. The information later led investigators to believe that it was a local, or at the very least acquainted with the region. In the course of her training, Mucklow kept him talking and when she inquired about what his hometown was He refused to reveal his origins to her. Then she took another approach and asked him "Do do you hold grudges towards Northwest?" This question appeared to be a surprise to him and he replied quietly, "I don't have a grudge against you airline Madame. I'm just a bit angry."

Then, Cooper's hand began to jerk up, possibly because of the tension which he was trying to cover up. He poured some of his drink from his glass. Mucklow was a bit frightened at first, awed by the sudden action. He then asked her to tell him what the exact time was. He was sure it was about 5:00, however, the fact that he was not wearing a watch. As he looked out the window, Mucklow noticed the fact that they had been "over Tacoma now", which indicated that he'd flown over this region of the country before and was well-versed in the area. When Mucklow informed Cooper it was just later than 5:00, he got anxious and asked her to confirm if Federal agents had tried to fool him. He then added that "they're not going to kill my life." Bewildered, Mucklow called the cockpit to find out what the issue was. Scott said that the two parachutes weren't there yet at the airport. He said "Ask Cooper if he would like to begin our descent without chutes in place." Cooper was Cooper was asked this, Cooper replied, "Yes." At 5:24 p.m. officials in the air let Scott know they had all the parachutes as well as the money (which was photographed and stored on microfilm to aid in attempts to track it) And then, a few minutes later the captain rang to the rear of the plane "The Front chutes have arrived located at the terminal. We're going down."

Chapter 9: The Ground And The Jump

"Out an unassuming doorway for service
To front of it, the plane
Cooper leapt into the dark
In the cold rain
They say that it is due to the colder wind.
It was 69 degrees below
There's not much chance the man would make it
But if he was, what did he do?" - The Ballad of D.B. Cooper

Cooper likely done some research on prior hijackings, and also studied the ways other hijackers were snuffed out by police because Cooper was given specific directions concerning what would transpire when he was on the ground. He first instructed Scott to drop the plane on a tarmac that was used away distance from where the principal building is and then demanded the pilot shut off all lights inside the aircraft, which could prevent shooting at him. This was a smart move since the FBI later acknowledged that "there was FBI agents equipped with scoped rifles that were ready to use if there were indications in place, to take him out."

Cooper had previously advised Northwest that they ought not allowed to come close to the plane using any kind of vehicle. Therefore, the person who was chosen to bring the parachutes and money was required to carry the weighty load on his feet. In addition this man was not a different person then Al Lee, Northwest Orient's Seattle operations manager. The Federal Aviation Agency official was present and was requested to join the plane to inform Cooper be aware of the dangers of hijacking an aircraft however, he declined the request.

In this moment, Cooper had grown most at ease with Mucklow. A fervent Christian Mucklow was capable of using her faith to calm her nerves as well as interact directly with Cooper on a more personal level. While Cooper didn't necessarily trust any person but their conversations had made him believe in her more than the rest in the group. He directed her to unlock the main door to the airplane, set up the stairs, and then wait for the airline employee at the bottom of the steps. With Cooper's piercing gaze she took the longest journey of her life.

She walked down the stairs and returned up the stairs carrying the cash bag.

As he saw the bill, Cooper grew angry; Cooper had specifically requested that the money was placed in a knapsack. It was an open bag. But he quickly recovered his composure and inspected the bills. As he gazed at Mucklow and his grin, he said, "Looks okay." In a flurry of anxiety, Mucklow joked, "There's plenty of money in the bag. Would you like to have some?" Taken aback, Cooper did indeed reach back inside the bag to give her a large amount of money. Confounded and embarrassed she mumbled, "Sorry, sir. There are no tips. Northwest Orient policy."

Then Cooper directed her to return down the steps and pick them up. If she complained that they'd not be able to handle the weight and he was rude to her, he cut her off and said, "They aren't that heavy. It shouldn't be a problem." This took two tripsbefore she was able to get the parachutes aboard. Then she pleaded for passengers' safety, begging, "Why not let them go? The crew is still there as well as the aircraft."

After everything he requested was in the plane, Cooper gave permission for the other passengers to get off the plane. He was able to watch them leave peacefully. all left "decently and in good order," before allowing Schaffner and another flight attendant to depart too. After being told they could leave they shocked him by seeking their wallets. Cooper smiled and said, "Sure, I'm not going to bite you." Then he looked at Schaffner and asked her to hold the bag to hold for a second. Much to his delight she lifted it off his palm before stating, "It is heavy."

When the women who were with them were leaving, Cooper again became angry at the time he realized that the fuel wasn't being delivered to the plane. Cooper was looking at Mucklow and demanded, "Close the shades." Then he began to complain about the plastic bag that federal agents had placed the money into. Before Mucklow realized what was going on, Cooper began cutting one of the parachutes and destroying the rope and fabric used to wrap the money into. While the authorities didn't know Cooper's actions had clarified that the second parachutes wouldn't be used to create an escape jump.

After having tied up his illegally obtained cash, Cooper became calm again and began to give his next set of directions for Mucklow: "We're going to Mexico City or anyplace in Mexico. Gear down, flaps down. The flaps can be trimmed to fifteen. There is a place in Mexico to refill your tank however, not here within America. United States. The cabin lights up, and no one can be within the first-class curtain...The forward door has to be opened and the staircase must be lowered."

These directions, particularly the specific reference to keeping the flaps of the wing at 15 degrees, suggested that Cooper was incredibly knowledgeable about aerodynamics as well as flying. Cooper even revealed to the pilot the altimeter was in his wrist that could be used to measure the altitude. But, these last instructions presented a challenge; after having consulted with the engineers of the airline the pilot informed Cooper that they were unable to safely take off without the staircase in the back down. Cooper was able to accept and said they could leave the staircase up during takeoff and as long as the pilot didn't pressurize their cabin when they were on the ground. At this point, Cooper obviously did not wish to be pulled out of the plane at the moment he lifted the forward steps.

While all this was happening it was evident that fueling was being completed and Cooper became more impatient. At the point, he moaned, "It shouldn't take this time." The moment he noticed the fuel truck pulling away and he was in the phone with the cockpit, shouting, "Let's get the show moving." To calm Cooper, Mucklow tried to give instructions on how to attach his parachutes. He waved away, screaming, "I don't need that." Then she requested that he let her move towards in the back of the airplane away from the place the pilot was about to open the door. He refused, but assured her that as soon as she demonstrated ways to lower the steps she would be able to join with the other crew members inside the cockpit. When Mucklow advised the pilot that she doesn't believe the stairs could be lower even when the plane was still in the air, he instantly made it clear and said she was mistaken that was a clear indication that he knew quite amount regarding this Boeing 727. Mucklow later explained steps to reduce the staircase, and also informed him that the plane was equipped with oxygen in the event that you'd need it. He responded, "Yes, I know the location. If I ever need it, I'll get the thing." He instructed her to turn off all lights in the plane.

As Cooper was once more upset that the plane wasn't going anywhere, Mucklow informed him that the pilots were working on their flight plans and he responded in a tense manner, "Never mind. It's possible to do this on the radio after we're up." Convinced that the time she spent with him was drawing to ending, Mucklow asked him one other question, and it was the one she was the most keen to get an respond to was: what was he planning to do about the explosive? After a long day of clear response from her captors she was a bit shaken by his indifferent answer: "Take it with me or take it down." But she didn't have time to think about it and he swiftly returned to her and stated, "Go to the cockpit. close the first-class curtains. You must ensure that no one comes out." The lady was all too pleased to follow the rules.

For one of the first times since he stepped on his plane Cooper took off his tie and removed the button at the top in his shirt. Cooper then used the parachute line the money in a secure knot to his chest. He then sat in front of the door as waiting for his plane to depart. After a short time about 7:45 p.m. the plane was soaring back into the sky, around two hours after it arrived in Seattle.

Cooper was patient until the plane's climb stabilized before turning off the switch that lowers the aft staircase and then it did fail. Disappointed, he called the cockpit to request assistance. However, before he received a response after a second time. The switch was activated and the stairs were raised which allowed the wind to blow throughout the cockpit. At this moment, the plane significantly and the ears started to pop inside the cockpit. As they heard the roaring sound from the cabin in front, Scott called and asked, "Can you hear me? What can we assist the situation?" Cooper replied tersely, "No." Another officer contacted him a couple of minutes later and inquired "Everything is okay?" Again, Cooper said, "Everything is okay."

In all the careful preparation that went in to the hijacking appears that Cooper did not think about the coldness it would take to leap from an airplane at that height and Cooper was about to fly free into -7°C air and icy cold rain. He was dressed in a simple business suit and loafers, shoes and raincoat. But the moment arrived and, regardless the fact that Cooper is cold, or not, he certainly believed it was time to turn back. As the plane flew just less than 200 miles per minute, Cooper was able to get out using two chutes, his money and his clothing (aside the tie). Cooper also took the "bomb" along with him or threw it away from the plane. After he stepped off the steps to jump, he stepped into the black abyss that was the stormy northwest Pacific night when lightning was the only source of light in the dark. According to Geoffrey Gray noted in New York magazine, "The cloud ceiling that night was 5,000 feet with some of the roughest land in the country was below it: pine forests and hemlock, spruce and spruce, canyons with bears and cougars and white-water rapids and lakes, all flowing out to the Pacific."

The plane made a smooth landing in Reno at around 10:15. This was about two hours after Cooper had jumped. The law enforcement authorities had tried to track Cooper's movements using two planes to track the hijacked aircraft from both sides but the plane's low speed made it difficult for Air Force's fighter jets. At the point that the plane that was slower used by the National Guard joined the chase and was believed to have been able to track Cooper's movements, Cooper was already jumping.

Chapter 10: In The Ground Or In It?

"Diving in the wild without having a strategy, and without the appropriate equipment, in such dire conditions, he may not have ever even had his 'chute' open." -- FBI Special Agent Larry Carr.

The moment he jumped and fell, the tale about D. B. Cooper was either over in a flash or continued into the subsequent stage. If it did end in a way that was accepted by a number of FBI agents and even Richard Tosaw, this is most likely how it took place: "Disoriented by the speed at which he fell, Cooper was unable to discover the rip cord, and his chute was unable to open. He may have found the rip cord however, he pulled it out in the wrong place and it became tangled around him. Or , his chute opened, but he could not determine the direction and speed of his fall, as he was unable to use the advanced military parachutes in favour of the more shaky manual chutes. In the end the chute was unable to stop the fall. Instead of gliding in a gentle manner to the ground, as his mind had it, he crashed to the ground until he fell unconscious due to shock and oxygen deprivation."

If Cooper was not able to survive the leap This is the most realistic way to describe the scenario as it indicates that Cooper was dead or unconscious when his body crashed into the ground, or perhaps an aquatic body like that of the Columbia River. There are many theories that suggest that the majority of the money that was attached to his body remained in his body when it was buried in the dark waters, and was transported downstream. When it was being swept along and tossed repeatedly against limbs and rocks, but some of it eventually broke free and washed up along the shore and was discovered in the year the year 1980. However, the bulk of the $200,000 was tangled in the parachute, as the body was pulled through in the water until it got stuck in a very deep location. In the following months those remains D. B. Cooper could have been transformed into fish food, and what was left could have been consumed in the process by bacteria. The result was only bones to be buried under silt at the bottom the river. According to Tosaw said later, "I'm convinced he's on the bottom of the Columbia River. I'm sure his skeleton will end up there and his parachutes, as well as the remainder of the money."

FBI agent Himmelsbach believes that, even Cooper survived the jump, Cooper initially made it to the top and landed safely, he would likely be injured when he hit the ground and probably wouldn't have survived for all that long "My impression is that he could have been injured regardless of the situation he fell into. I'm thinking that Cooper generally walked to the edge of a stream. Cooper didn't have water sources, and didn't carry any He would've needed to be able to drink water in order to survive. Therefore, I believe that he walked to the creek, and died there."

Captain Scott was also of the opinion that no one would have survived a fall from this height at such a horrible time. Although he was unable to speak with the media, shortly after his death, his widow told to a reporter "He was afraid he would fall in Lake Merwin and got tangled in dead trees, and fell to the ground and died." There's a lot of evidence that supports Scott's assertion and most notable is the story that was told by Elsie Rodgers of Cozad, Nebraska. She would often delight her children with tales of her discovery of a skull of a person on the banks of Columbia River in Washington State. They were both awestruck and shocked when, few days after her demise they discovered an unidentified skull tucked hidden in a hatbox within her attic. Her children immediately handed over their skulls over to FBI however, the Bureau could not come to any conclusion regarding its source.

It's not surprising that many Americans were hopeful that Cooper lived to see. Americans in the early 1970s were adamant about the anti-hero and for many, D. B. Cooper was not a thief, but an hero. In the end, he did not harm anyone and had smashed the right blow for people of all ages against the big businesses. In fact, should he make it through, he would have had plenty of people help him avoid the police. For as one law-abiding citizen said, "You know, it's hilarious. People are actually cheering for this guy. This is all anyone wants to discuss. I have heard it over and over. Hope he got it. the man is deserving, wish he's able to get rid of every penny. As if he's some sort like a Robin Hood character. The man is John Doe. He wasn't some radical ... It was just you or your neighbour." Historical historian Walt Crowley agreed, telling the Seattle Times, "It's that mysterious mystique. It was an astonishingly bold action to lower that rear gangway to the ground and leap into the dark and stormy night. It didn't harm anyone ... as well, and everyone loves a mysterious story."

The FBI's principal detective, Ralph Himmelsbach, disagreed and called Cooper "a pest," "a bastard," "a filthy, corrupt criminal" and "nothing else than devious, corrupt criminal who put at risk the lives of over 40 people in exchange for money." If anyone didn't know what he meant with his remarks, he then added "That's certainly not an act of heroism. It's selfish, risky and an antisocial act. I don't admire his character at all. He's not awe-inspiring at all. He's just greedy and stupid." In a way that is less inflamed, Himmelsbach noted, "When such a person goes out of view, the people surrounding him are thrilled and don't think too much about it, possibly thinking they're in jail once more. It's not likely to happen to an older man of 48 who's been living a normal existence in the past, and suddenly do something like this guy did."

Himmelsbach believes that Cooper died in the jump or shortly thereafter but it didn't stop him from scouring the area, hunting each tip that would appear. He admitted, "Every so often one (of these) would pop up and I'd experience the adrenaline rush. There's a man at a bar, carrying several $20 bills He's struggling on one foot and somebody asks him where the roll came from and he tells them he may have hijacked an aircraft. It's easy to track them down and they go out."

A parachute expert thinks Cooper might have survived , and put his chances at 50 percent. Frank Heyl offered some alternatives: "Let's say he went to the bottom of the ocean. It is essential to know how to use the parachute. It can be used to float. The life expectancy of the man will not be very long in the water. It's cold, and you have to think about the season of year it was in, which means Cooper probably had only a short amount of time to reach the shore. However, I believe he could have completed this." In response to those who believe Cooper was not prepared and unexperienced, Heyl added, "We aren't sure what he put on in the suit, but he could have been wearing an underwear set which he definitely should have. Also, what was in his pockets might be the most crucial aspect because it could have provided him the survival tools. If a man had a knife, a lighter from a cigarette, and clothes he wears, you could have stayed out in the wild. It's possible. I'm thinking he may have buried the chute. I believe he may have put the briefcase in the ground. He probably disposed of it. I believe he put the money into his coat and then went to a city somewhere and got lost."

If Cooper did survive the jump His first priority would have been to get through the night. When he finally landed at around 8:15 in the evening, and a storm was in full force. He could have unhooked his parachutes , and most likely attempted to conceal them, which would be quite an effort. With nothing other than hands, his best option was to cover them with underbrush or even sink them if he was close to a body of water. After that the man would have had to find a place to stay for the night. This would not be easy at all. The trees of Northwest Northwest tend to be straight and tall with branches that rise above, which means they could not have provided any kind of shelter. Actually, they would be lightning magnets, and especially hazardous to be around during the midst of a storm.

If Cooper was alive, he would be required to trek from the beginning. Then the need to think of that a hunt would soon be going on, but in reality there was no manhunt in the morning because of circumstances in the climate. There could have been a variety of issues hindering Cooper's ability to hike for instance, his shoes. Cooper had been wearing business loafers at the time Parachutists generally prefer tight-laced boots or athletic shoes to jump in since the force of fall can take regular shoes off their feet. Therefore, Cooper might or might not have put any shoes to walk in. The second issue was direction. Since Cooper did not have an alarm clock, it is unlikely that he would have thought to carry the compasses. Even in the event that you did, you'd have not the luxury of knowing where he was at the time the jump occurred, and therefore it is unlikely that he could have determined the right direction to travel in.

There is a possibility that Cooper was actually walking through the Northwest wilderness in a suit of business attire and loafers while carrying around $200,000 of cash. However, the trek might have been affected due to an injury, as even experienced and skilled jumpers are prone to ankle injuries at some point during their career. Cooper's chute did not have a mechanism to stop it from moving as it hit the ground which is why he could have hit the ground hard and might have broken bones. This could make getting out of this forest harder however it wasn't impossible.

Chapter 11: The Case Against

Simply because Hunt is in line with D.B. Cooper's age body, build, and facial characteristics have the same experience and special information to be Cooper and had various motives to pull off the heist; a reason to believe that he was invincible with a similar mode of operationalis, does not mean that he is Cooper. In the end, some discrepancies or flaws in the Hunt-was Cooper theory suggest doubt on Hunt's claim to be the infamous sky pirate. Therefore, let's tackle the issues head on and see how Hunt's Hunt stands against them.

1. Cooper was brown-eyed. Hunt's eyes were blue. When one reads the document that the FBI first published describing D.B. Cooper within the descriptions of his eyes, it says "possibly brown." The "possibly" qualification was added with good reason. Of the dozen witnesses who saw Cooper only one of them said they noticed the color of his eyes. This is because Cooper had a pair of glasses over his eyes when he had set the scene. The person who recognized his eye color was stewardess Flora Schaffner

who was standing in front of Cooper for the brief time they spent together, which is not the ideal position from which to view. In addition, the majority of their interactions involved opening up and displaying the bomb in the suitcase. Schaffner's attention was centered on the bomb, and calming the person in the seat, not how his eyes were colored. Another thing to take into consideration is the fact that the flight occurred in the late afternoon, and also after a heavy rainstorm that made the interior dark and dimly lit plane, not the best conditions to gauge the color of eyes.

The lighting conditions impact how people see colors, and so does the distance between the person who is watching and the object to be watched. Witnesses have reported Cooper's hair color as black, brown and jet black and his suit's color was described as brown, black, and russet.

Some ophthalmologists believe that the color of eyes can be dependent on the hue of clothes a person wears. When light is reflected off the iris, the surrounding colors can reflect off of it and make blue-eyed people's eyes appear to be brown. If Cooper actually was wearing a brown-colored dark-colored suit, this may very likely have created the illusion that the eyes of Cooper were dark even though they were not.

2.Cooper was an olive-colored man. Hunt is Caucasian. Many witnesses have described Cooper as being slim or sporting an olive complexion. Schaffner as well as Alice Hancock both used the words "olive complexion" when they testified to the FBI which makes it appear as if Cooper was of some other ethnicity than Caucasian. Schaffner even speculated that Cooper was an Latino as did the other passenger Robert Gregory. However, Tina Mucklow, who spent more time with Cooper than anyoneelse, first stated his skin tone as medium. She also described the race of Cooper as white. Also, witnesses Bill Mitchell. There were no other witnesses who could have guessed that Cooper had been a Latino.

It's possible that the dim lighting conditions in the aircraft caused some witnesses to perceive Cooper's complexion as olive, and his ethnicity as Latino (a hypothesis that was among the witness who was mentioned within one of the FBI accounts). A different possibility would be prior to when the FBI was able to speak with witnesses, the witness's discussed what happened with them, and compared notes, and one witness's memory of an olive-colored complexion filtered through the memories of the other witnesses.

Another possible scenario is Cooper put on the makeup that made his skin darker, but in the event that this was the case, it's hard to believe that Mucklow didn't notice it in the time she spent with Cooper.

Perhaps Cooper might have had a nice tanning. In the majority of his life, Hunt was an outdoorsman and his skin displayed signs of sun-induced damage. Hunt spent a lot of time in South America and Miami, in which his skin could be sunk into a puddle of. Photographs of color of Hunt that were taken following the Watergate period reveal him to possess a bronze skin tone. In the end in a memoir called Mission Impossible that Watergate burglar Eugenio Martinez wrote following his imprisonment and wrote about Hunt, "There was something peculiar about this person. His tan, you'll remember isn't like the tan of someone who's at the beach."

Whatever the reason whatever the reason, the FBI sketch drawn from the statements of the stewardesses just after the incident isn't likely to indicate a person who is who is Latino ethnicity.

3.Cooper had reached his mid-forties , and Hunt aged 53 during the time the crime was committed. Hunt had turned 53 the month prior to Cooper's caper. Cooper caper. The guesses about Cooper's age varied widely. Two witnesses suggested the age of Cooper was 35, while another estimated him to be in his early fifties as did the attendants on board. believed they were in the late to mid-forties. Based on the transcripts compiled from the conversations of the flight crew in the moment that Florence Schaffner alerted the officers that the plane had been hijacked, she informed them that the person responsible for the hijack was in his 50s. For Hunt who was physically active and in decent health.

4.The FBI suspected Cooper was an area resident. Hunt is from New York and D.C.

regions. The belief of Cooper and the FBI of the fact that Cooper was from Washington or Oregon was based on an assumption and a few observations. It was believed that nobody in their good conscience would leap over the vast, remote, wooded region unless they were acquainted with it. Furthermore, he'd had an easier time getting back residence before anyone noticed he was missing if he was located near the site of the landing. What about the observations? The flight Cooper was able to see Seattle-Tacoma from the air. He also knew that the military base had been established located about 20 miles from Seattle.

Let's begin with the assertions regarding Cooper noting Seattle. If Cooper had been flying into Seattle prior to then It's likely that it would have been a city he recognized through the skies. Hunt had a habit of frequent flyer and it's very likely that he'd flew to Northwest Orient from that very airport. In 1955, Hunt as well as his entire family moved to Japan. In 1955 the only two airlines that operated flights to in the U.S. to Japan were Pan Am and Northwest Orient.

Northwest Orient had two hubs that connected to Japan. The more direct route was from Minnesota. However, leaving that hub required crossing Canada and making several stops on the route. The Seattle hub was, however it offered a direct unstop service to Japan. As Hunt's primary story at the time included the fact that he'd become a wealthy American It's more likely that he would have chosen the less direct and more appealing route.

There's also evidence to suggest he'd flown in the Northwest Orient. The novel House Dick, he makes mention of a character who had an Northwest toothbrush. The novel "One of Our Agents is Missing (1967) the story starts in the form of an CIA protagonist (clearly inspired by Hunt) traveling to Japan via the Northwest Orient flight.

It's also possible that Cooper may have targeted Seattle in part because he knew some local financial institutions had at the very least $200,000 lying around , waiting to be seized.

In the context of Cooper's awareness the existence of an air base situated close by, it's not odd that someone who was part of the air corps of the army in World War II (as did Hunt) and also in the CIA would know the locations of air force bases were .

Let's look at the idea that Cooper was able to leap across the Washington wilderness because Cooper was familiar with the area. In the event that Cooper did have an associate or accomplices , and a plan for retrieval then the location of the wilderness wouldn't be as important. In the heists Hunt carried out along with Liddy, Hunt enlisted the assistance of Cuban exiles who were eager to aid Hunt to aid in enduring Communism. Hunt's friend Bernie Barker, who had relations with airlines operating located in Miami, Haiti, and the Dominican Republic, helped in both of the operations. It's likely that he helped Hunt out during the NORJAK Heist had Hunt wanted to do so help, particularly since Hunt mentioned that he needed money to fund a business idea which he as well as Barker were trying to establish.

5.Hunt's appearance was advertised in major newspapers, and his face and voice were broadcast on the television throughout his Watergate hearings. What is the reason that no witnesses came forward to confirm Hunt as Cooper and Cooper? The same question can be asked of other D.B. Cooper suspects as they all have at one point seen their pictures published in magazines or on TV. In the Hunt case Hunt there is evident reasons to believe that the witnesses were afraid to testify.

Imagine that you're Tina Mucklow. You've been held captive for three hours by an criminal who is armed with an explosive. Then , seven months later, the identity of Cooper is revealed as the Watergate report comes out. Based on news reports, you discover that Cooper is an aide to The most influential man in the world , and is or was a member of the CIA. In addition, Cooper knows your name as well as your employer and (thanks to reports in the press) the city you live in. If he's looking to shut you down Cooper or his gang aren't likely to have any trouble in locating you.

One of the issues that you'll be thinking about in your head at this moment is the possibility that the incident was a black ops job of the CIA or carried out for the President's benefit as crazy as they might appear in the past, would have placed the whole thing in a different perspective. At the time, in the beginning of Watergate there were serious questions about whether or it was the CIA was the culprit behind the break-in. If the Agency was responsible for the heist then it wouldn't be absurd to believe that it was involved in the NORJAK Heist too.

Keep in mind that by this time, the CIA was beginning to earn an image of being involved in some shady actions. Therefore, witnesses who identify an CIA officer as D.B. Cooper might be infuriate those who are not the right people. One could also ask if it is possible that the FBI was working in conjunction with the CIA and this whole affair was a huge ploy to deceive people in the American people. The most secure option is to not say anything and to simply dismiss any other theories the FBI proposes.

There's also the possibility that Cooper was threatening the witness, with evidence that suggests this took place. in Skyjack, Geoffrey Gray recounts a fascinating story that Stewardess Florence Schaffner recounts to

Cooper. According to Schaffner's account of events, shortly following the NORJAK incident the man began following her around, appearing whenever she went, and later being seen with her on the plane. When she confronted him the man claimed he'd seen D.B. Cooper in prison, and that Cooper wanted to speak with her. She resisted, prompting the man to state that Cooper was in Bay of Pigs and in the CIA.

Was Schaffner trying to convey to Gray an indication that she was aware of Cooper's identity Cooper and also that she was Hunt? In Gray's version, Schaffner's account doesn't provide an accurate time frame for what time the stalker's incident was actually happening in March, however by the time of 1973, Hunt was in fact imprisoned. He began a testimony during the Watergate hearings several months later, which would be the time when Hunt was most worried about witnesses being able to recognize his name.

In Gray's memoir, Schaffner tells Gray she believes that Cooper had threatened Tina Mucklow, and that's why Mucklow was able to hide from the media following the incident. She then quit work as a Stewardess becoming the convent.

To add to the anxiety In addition, as Hunt became a well-known public name and conspiracy theorists began to accuse Hunt of having been connected to the Kennedy assassination, based on Hunt's alleged resemblance to a transient who was detained in Dallas close to the site that the murder took place.

It is the truth that of the four witnesses, it was the FBI was most interested in: Mucklow, Schaffner, William Mitchell and Alice Hancock. However, all of them except Hancock began to recluse herself to an degree.

It's also fascinating to see how Hunt managed the media attention after the Watergate report came out. When Hunt as well as the other conspirators went to court on the 19th of September in 1972 the five burglars, as well as G. Gordon Liddy all were dressed in suits and tie. Hunt was similarly dressed but he was wearing sunglasses to shield the eyes, a bizarre panama hat that covered one's head and a cigar firmly inserted between his teeth. Although it's possible that he just been trying to conceal his identity from friends however, with his unique name, it appears it was an ineffective exercise.

When the Watergate hearings started at the time of the Watergate hearings, the B sketches of the witnesses were released which was the image that the majority of Americans were now seeing of Cooper. The B sketches do not look like Hunt.

The man was fond of wearing sunglasses. At the Watergate hearings, there were photos of him in black suits and wearing sunglasses. Why is it necessary to wear sunglasses in the first place? One asks. Are his eyes so sensitive? It's almost as if Hunt was consciously trying to look like Cooper. Being aware that he was on TV did he want to communicate with Cooper or any Cooper witnesses who may be able to recognize the man?

Another thing. When Hunt was called to testify at the hearings, Hunt was no longer the person he was before. The grief of losing his family and wife and being in prison took its toll. He looks gaunt and swollen. One year later, when he began promoting the memoir he wrote, Undercover, he looks like a completely different person looking younger and larger than the Hunt who testified in his testimony at the Watergate hearings. There's a good chance that there was enough time by that participants in his Cooper Heist (especially those who had never seen his eyes) would not have noticed the man.

6.If Hunt's aversion to Communism as well as the Cuban skyjackings was a motivating factor, then why doesn't he refer to the skyjackings on his memoirs? The memoirs were all published some time from that Cooper heist. It is certain that if Hunt were really Cooper and he was, he wouldn't have been able to draw interest to any thing that could be associated with Cooper. Cooper heist. Making a fuss about the planes that were hijacked and then taken to Cuba would have done exactly the opposite. In actual fact When Hunt describes the aftermath of the Bay of Pigs debacle in Give Us this Day, Hunt discusses issues such as the building of the Berlin Wall, the missile crisis, and the war that was raging across Latin America, but leaves out the raging of hijackings, both in and out of Cuba which followed. It's a noticeable absence.

7.D.B. Cooper was an Canadian. The theory was reportedly developed by Tom Kaye and his team at Citizen Sleuths. The theory originated from three elements: Dan Cooper being an identical name to an Belgium superhero from comic books (so Cooper is French Canadian), Cooper speaks English without accent (okay it's isn't French Canadian), and Cooper's claim of requesting negotiable American currency in exchange for his cash. If someone American was requesting money, would he utilize such an odd phrase to mean "negotiable American currency?" Wouldn't it sound more like something that a foreigner might be saying? Not necessarily. "Negotiable" refers to financial instruments that must be reported by people traveling to or from different countries. It could be a mistake committed by a citizen of an overseas country that is used to exchanging foreign currency in exchange for American dollars or vice versa, but it could as easily be a remark used by an American who has traveled to other countries often and was required the need to swap American currency in exchange for foreign currency, and the reverse.

Hunt was, in reality often leave for overseas while working for the CIA in addition to the fact that , he and his family went to Europe at times. The error only suggests that a person who travels exchanges American currency at times like Hunt.

8.Cooper was a bourbon drinker and also consumed Raleigh cigarettes. Hunt used to smoke a pipe and was an avid Scotch man. According to his autobiography, Hunt appears to be going far to make sure the fact that his preferred drink would always be Scotch. It's also well-known that Hunt smoked pipe tobacco and cigars, but not Raleigh cigarettes. In any case, Raleigh cigarettes were smoked by those who could not afford more expensive. This wouldn't be Hunt.

The problem in this claim is the fact that Hunt was trained by both the OSS as well as in the CIA on ways to hide his identity. If he was looking to throw the FBI off the scent then he'd know better than to smoke Scotch and drink pipes under the name of D.B. Cooper.

However maybe he was a fan of Bourbon. The Hunt story One one of our Agents is Missing The CIA character is based on Hunt is a drinker of bourbon, not Scotch.

9.Why did Florence Schaffner and Tina Mucklow confirm that Tina Mucklow and Florence Schaffner identified Hunt to be Cooper when Hunt was killed in 2007? The most likely explanation could be that neither woman was willing to confess that they had known Cooper's identity Cooper from the time of when they were at the Watergate hearings, even if they had recognized him. If they thought Hunt was working under the direction under the CIA, Schaffner and Mucklow could have also feared reprisal from the Agency in the event that they revealed that Cooper was a career man within the Agency.

10.Florence Schaffner's 1988 sketch doesn't look like Hunt. It was in 1988 that the makers of the television series Unsolved Mysteries had Schaffner sit together with a sketcher and try to draw an exact sketch using her 17-year-old memory. The result was a picture of a man sporting the Nixonian widow's peak an enormous nose, and prominent cheekbones. The drawing was in no way similar to any of the sketches earlier or even to E. Howard Hunt. However, Schaffner was always an exception in the sense of what witnesses believed Cooper appeared to be. Three stewardesses met Roy Rose to produce the initial drawing, Alice Hancock and Tina Mucklow were both pleased with the drawing. Schaffner did not. In the year following, when the FBI made a sketch like the one that Schaffner had in his memory, Schaffner said it was "an outstanding resemblance." However, the sketch as well as that of the Unsolved Mysteries drawing look nothing similar, and it is reasonable to believe that Schaffner's memory was affected sometime in the past, which resulted in a sketch that might not have been as similar to Cooper in any way.

Chapter 12: Norjak

"The FBI learned of the incident in the air and immediately initiated an extensive investigation which lasted several years. The FBI referred to it as NORJAK to refer to the Northwest hijacking, our team questioned many people. We followed leads throughout the country and looked through the plane for evidence. By the five-year anniversary of the hijacking, we'd considered more than 800 suspects and eliminated all but two dozen from consideration."

"I must confess that if I was planning to search for Cooper I'd go to Cooper's home in Washougal." - FBI Chief Investigator Ralph Himmelsbach

The investigation into the identity of D. B. Cooper was and what was he doing started the moment Captain Scott called the tower and informed them the he was being hacked. In the end, by the time Cooper was able to jump into the air, the FBI was familiar with the situation and the investigation was in full swing. When the passengers were released after the jump, the FBI brought them all together and read the roll of the manifest of passengers. Each by one, hands moved up until the agent came to one of the names on the roster. When he announced Dan Cooper's number Dan Cooper, there was no response. He repeated the name repeatedly, but no one did anything. Dan Cooper was the hijacker.

Then, the top FBI agent in Portland started receiving calls from journalists and asking for details about the identity of the person suspected. Clyde Jabin, a reporter for United Press International, thought that he had heard "D. B. Cooper". Unable to comprehend what was being said in the line's dynamic, Jabin asked, "D as in dog, and B which means Boy?" Distracted by weightier things, the agent replied "Right" and left. Jabin was then the one to reveal the name D. B. Cooper to the world.

The 35 people who Cooper was released from were confused rather than scared They were unsure of the truth until they were confronted by agents who wanted their declarations. The main problem was what Cooper was like, as the statements of Schaffner and others who had been around Cooper were not in agreement on this aspect. Cooper was clearly Caucasian in his appearance and was male however, in addition, reports were a bit ambiguous and inconsistent like eyewitness accounts typically are. Initial reports stated that Cooper was aged between 30-50 years old, 5'8-6 tall, had brown eyes (Schaffner was the only person who could see him without his dark glasses) Dark black hair and wore either a black or brown suit.

It was the next huge leap after Flight 305 landed in Reno, Nevada. It wasn't until that the plane was safely landed that Captain Scott realized that the last passenger actually jump. After he had signaled the tower to give the all-clear the crew and he were attacked by FBI agents, who would end in finding only two parachutes, Cooper's tie, as well as a few of his cigarettes butts.

The parachutes that was left on the plane along with the bag that it was placed in.

While agents led the crew of the plane off for interrogation, a lot of passengers climbed aboard and were laden down using cameras, evidence collecting kits. The photographers were first on the scene to take pictures of all the areas of the plane and making certain to capture close-ups of the area where Cooper was sitting in the staircase in the back and the lounge for the stewardess. These were also the very first to spot the main clue Cooper didn't bring along with him the black tie clip with the distinct tie clips. After taking several pictures to document the location of the tie and where it was found, the agent stood back and let a colleague to grab the tie. After a brief exam, he put it into an evidence box and labeled the item with his initials as well as the date and location it was located. The tie was later found to be an important element in the investigation because although DNA testing was several years away and the agents were able to collect enough skin cells from the clip to eventually create a DNA sample. Although the evidence isn't definitively identified a suspect but it has cleared several people who claimed to be as being D. B. Cooper.

When the photographer made his way through in the plane, an officer using the fingerprint kit accompanied him closely, cleaning the armrests, magazines, and door knobs to collect prints. Cooper was not wearing gloves while on the plane, and was not concerned with leaving footprints. This could suggest that he was not in legal trouble before or was a member of the military, in which case his fingerprints could have been in a file somewhere. As with the DNA extracted by the clip the fingerprints have been ruled out as suspects , but not definitively identifying any.

Alongside the fingerprint tech was a team of other agents looking for evidence. Each napkin, bag and glass was sealed and identified, with particular concentration given to objects that were closest to the spot the spot where Cooper was in his seat. Alongside the two glasses he was drinking his bourbon and bourbons from, investigators located eight Raleigh cigarettes that he left behind. The choice of his drink and the the brand of cigarette would turn out to be significant elements of evidence to narrow down the suspects.

While agents were interrogating witnesses, while others were gathering evidence, another group of G-Men was conducting the search, which was to start at dawn the following morning. They interrogated Scott and his team extensively to discover as close as they could to the exact moment they experienced the shift within the rear part of the airplane. The general consensus, confirmed later by a replay of the incident is that the shimmy in the rear they felt was felt after Cooper opened the stairway and then jumped. With the aid of maps, rulers and a lot of pencil leads They determined what they thought was Cooper's most likely landing point and decided that this was the place they'd begin their search once the sun rose.

One topic of discussion during the evening was the specifics of what they were searching for whether it was a fugitive, or a body. The majority of the jumpers who had been trained to call in was that they'd probably come across a dead body. The military plane close behind Flight 305 when it left Seattle-Tacoma didn't see Cooper jump and was not aware that any chute opening. Although they might miss it in the dim and almost moonless night, it added credibility to the notion that Cooper's parachutes never opened. Others suggested that, even if the parachute had been opened, the forest the man was jumping into was so dense that Cooper was more likely to get caught in a tree rather than landing on the ground. Whatever the case, the only thing that everyone could be certain about that night is that it would discover Cooper alive or dead. As it transpired the probe they been naming NORJAK (the abbreviation of the FBI for "Northwest hijacking") was just getting started.

A map that is used by authorities to determine the location Cooper might have landed.

At dawn on the 25th of November The morning of November 25, Ralph Himmelsbach, a licensed pilot who flew around and back for the duration of the day in the region where Cooper was believed to have bailed out. Bureau believed Cooper had escaped. He did not see a drainage in the trees and no floating body in a river or lake and no smoke from a campfire and there was no one moving around. When he finished the day it was over and delighted to land however, he knew that whatever that he couldn't discover from the air would likely be discovered quickly from the ground by the crew.

But the people who were on the ground were faced with a task waiting for them. Split into six teams that covered around 6 square miles, the agents trekked through the bushes and the men, who were wearing heavy coats and boots might have been wondering how a person dressed in Cooper's clothing could get through such dense underbrush. Their legs quickly became tired of fighting the pull of brambles and weeds, and their eyes got tired of looking on the dirt in dim light, as even when it was midday, time of day, dense trees over blocked the majority of the sun's rays.

The agents were assisted by police personnel from the surrounding area familiar with conducting searches in this area and had a few words of wisdom to share. However, even these officers became frustrated when the snow began to fall. "You've got to keep looking directly downwards," said one. "It definitely limits the possibility of being able to see something." The sheriff suggested, "If he was smart enough to have planned it this far, he surely isn't going to put the parachute in the air to be found." A FBI agent replied with a grim face, "We're either looking for the parachute, or perhaps an opening within the earth."

Soon, the law enforcement officers were not the only ones looking around the forest. Since Cooper being missing, and the fate of his disappearance undetermined many people started pouring into the area around, either because of curiosity or desire. It was a time when the American business was in a bad condition at the time and many thought of finding the money and then making quick getaways using the money. According to an elderly farmer "Even an honest Christian guy (would retain the funds). A large portion of the people living who live in Clark Country are having to be on welfare because they have lost their jobs. A man can buy a nice farm with this amount of money - even if he needed to move for Australia." Some were also those looking to make a real profit by getting the $25,000 reward that the airline offered for the information that led the way to cooper's arrest.

Within a few days, the probe began its next phase that was the crank letters. It is believed that Cooper or, more likely, someone who was pretending that he was him had a blast the game of teasing his accusers. One letter warned, "I must ask you"Who do you believe you to be, and what is it that you believe you're doing. I've pulled from one of the more successfuland known crime that we have today...No one was in danger and the perpetrator was determined to prove to the unbelievers of the public that a perfect crime could happen. There was no harm done." A different letter paints an even more tragic, than beautiful image, and stated, "I didn't rob Northwest Orient because I believed it was romantic or heroic, or any other terms that be associated with situations that carry high risk. There is no the modern day Robin Hood. Unfortunately, (I) do have 14 months of my life left. My entire life was one of haters as well as turmoil, hunger, and more hatred. This was the most efficient and fastest way to achieve some tranquility."

Similar to the Cooper case authorities were forced to handle copies of hijackings and once those who attempted to hijack were arrested They were often questioned in the hopes of establishing a connection to the Cooper incident. McCoy's hijacking, which occurred a few months later was comparable to Cooper's, so McCoy was identified as possibly D.B. Cooper and several subsequent books have been written that claim Cooper could be "the McCoy who was the real McCoy".

One of the people who the FBI interviewed was a seasoned skydiver. This was the person who manned the four chutes that were offered to Cooper. They learned some fascinating information from the man. The most important thing is that of the four chutes available, Cooper made a very poor decision. The primary chute was difficult to move, and the second chute wasn't an actual chute at all; Cooper admitted that he unintentionally given the airline employee who was preparing the parachutes to be an unintentional dummy chute. It was utilized in jumping training, but it was not able to be used, and Cooper did not have a functional chute at the time he went to jump.

The next question agents were interested in was whether Cooper was able to survive the fall. The skydiver was confident that Cooper may have survived, but probably not without injury. With the kind of chute he picked most likely, he was able to sustain some form severe injury or damage to either or both ankles (as the parachutist who was injured later said of the matter, "I think he's gotta be dead or the most fortunate human ever.") With this latest element of evidence the FBI warned all local hospitals to keep an eye out for anyone suffering from a broken leg or ankle.

Chapter 13: A Mystery Continues

An FBI image of the suspect illustrating his possible age change throughout the years.

"When the plane he was on board to Portland, Oregon last night the plane was a regular passenger, who identified himself as D. B. Cooper. Today, after he hijacked the plane of Northwest airlines jet, and robbing the passengers of Seattle and then taking off via parachute somewhere between the city to Reno, Nevada, the name given by one wire service was:"Master Criminal." Walter Cronkite

"The FBI says it has conducted an extensive search of more than 1,200 suspects, and collected enough documentation and case reports to fill out a 727." David Krajicek

On the 5th of December 1971, the unsuccessful hunt was coming to a close. Although the FBI had their top agents and the latest technology in place, neither would stand up to the rigors of winter's approaching. In the morning, the team informed the headquarters in Washington office: "For information of Bureau the terrain of the search area is different from a ridgeline that averages 17 hundred feet, and dense wood with a dense undergrowth...There are numerous hills and streams, and a lot of the forest is impervious. The air search was concluded with negative results. Eight hundred square miles were covered during this search. It was a negative results. It was also noted that the area is primarily composed of extremely rough terrain, with many roadways for logging in terrible state." In this sense the area they had been looking for was nearly too to handle to FBI field agents and specially trained police officers. What is the chance an individual wearing business attire and loafers have of making it out alive?

As the holiday season was coming up and the men fatigued and exhausted, it was the right time to put down the hunt and allow the natural process to unfold. A local police officer said "Come the next deer season, a hunter will locate Cooper." At an esoteric scale, the police officer was right, for although no one has located Cooper however, the first item of proof was discovered by a hunter in the year 1978.

This was an instructions card for lowering the stairs in the rear of a 727. it was discovered lying on an old logging road in Castle Rock, Washington. Although Cooper may have had this placard with his palm when he fell from the sky , or perhaps put it into his pocket to keep as a memento however, it is most likely to have fallen from the aircraft as the stairs were being lowered and fell to the ground without a trace.

The searchers returned in Spring of 1972 however, they did not have the same luck as the initial searches a few months prior. After being unable to find his men for several weeks an army colonel was forced to give his troops an opportunity to rest, and directed his assistant to leave an explanation message: "Due to near exhaustion of troops in the army, who have endured the rigors of rain snow, sleet and other severe weather conditions while traversing treacherous difficult, hilly brush and tree-covered areas in which Lieutenant. Colonel. Bonsell believes that for the soldiers their safety and welfare that they need to be resting and will suspend search for a short period of time." The troops were able to try again in the future, but they were again prevented by weather.

The months that were to follow, the physical search for the landing spot was a failure as the Bureau turned its attention to conducting follow-up on the various leads that were sent to them however, the majority of them were bogus and the few plausible possibilities never came to fruition. As the economy slumped, it continued to decline as did public respect for law enforcement agencies and the government and, in the general population people who pay any interest to the case in any way were not the kind of people who would have been likely to vote Cooper out. Although the case was open, slowly decreased in importance.

In the end, the FBI received its first real break almost 10 years after. In February of 1980 an individual living in Vancouver, Washington contacted them and handed over three bundles of money that they discovered on the banks of the Columbia River, about 40 miles downstream from the area that the FBI initially searched. When discussing this evidence the Special Agent

Carr was later to admit that "The true mystery lies in the money. The mystery surrounding the money is more fascinating that the puzzle about whom Cooper was. If you can unravel the amount of money, it can lead one to Cooper. It's all about money. The money is our sole chance." One thing that has afflicted those who worked for them, and is still it, is that none the money ever came up , except for three wet bags.

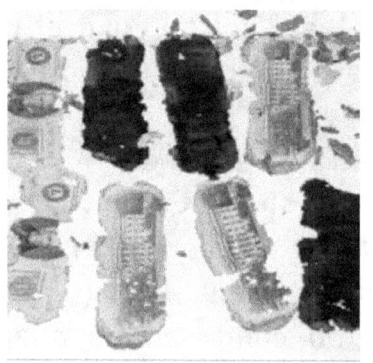

A photograph of the ransom money found in the year 1980.

Forty decades later, the biggest issue is: where are we with D. B. Cooper now? The person who was responsible for one of the biggest and most well-known hijackings of all time has passed away. If he did survive the jump and lived every moment of his existence extent, Cooper is now in his 80s. Even though it's still seen by authorities as strange that no ransom money has ever been found except for the money found in the Columbia River, some have suggested that Cooper may have been able to launder his cash at one of the numerous casinos that started appearing around the world in the late 1970s. property owned by Native American tribes. Perhaps D.B. Cooper passed away peacefully in the midst of a devoted family that was unaware of details about their loved one's unresolved background. The same thing was the case with Kenny Christiansen, a man who is often referred to as a suspect. Christiansen bought a house using cash in the few days after the incident, and passed away at the age of 94, and left over $200,000 at his bank, in addition to an impressive stamp and gold coin collection. Himmelsbach has dismissed Christiansen as an suspect, in part because it was a member of the airline that was hijacked: "We had an awful amount of comments from individuals who claimed this is an insider job. It's impossible because of a variety of reasons. The most obvious, if one knows the procedure of an airline is that it's not feasible for a conspiracy to develop because the participants are not in charge of which flights they're taking on...If you had any contact like I was with a lot of the employees who work in the industry of airline They are extraordinary people.

www.ingramcontent.com/pod-product-compliance
Lightning Source LLC
Chambersburg PA
CBHW050402120526
44590CB00015B/1792